D0355803
Edgar Allan Poe
THE UNKNOWN POE

An extremely rare French etching of Poe produced at the end of the nineteenth century

THE UNKNOWN POE

an anthology
of fugitive writings by Edgar Allan POE,
with
appreciations by Charles BAUDELAIRE,
Stephane MALLARMÉ, Paul VALÉRY,
J.K. HUYSMANS & André BRETON.

Edited by Raymond FOYE

City Lights

First Printing October 1980

Grateful acknowledgments:

"Edgar Poe by André Breton," from *Anthologie de L'Humour Noir*, copyright by Société Nouvelle des Editions Jean-Jacques Pauvert.

"On Poe" from *Situation de Baudelaire*. Paul Valéry, *The Collected Works in English*, Bollingen Series XLV. Vol. 8, *Leonardo, Poe, Mallarmé*, trans. Malcolm Cowley and James R. Lawler, © 1972 by Princeton University Press. Reprinted by permission of Princeton University Press.

Library of Congress Cataloging in Publication Data

Edgar Allan Poe, the unknown Poe.

1. Poe, Edgar Allan, 1809-1849—Criticism and interpretation—Addresses, essays, lectures. 2. Criticism—France—Addresses, essays, lectures.
I. Foye, Raymond, 1957- II. Poe, Edgar Allan, 1809-1849.
PS2638.E3 818'.309 80-24321
ISBN 0-87286-110-4 (pbk.)

CITY LIGHTS BOOKS are edited by Lawrence Ferlinghetti & Nancy Peters at the City Lights Bookstore, 261 Columbus Avenue, San Francisco, California 94133

CONTENTS

ILLUSTRATIONS

PREFACE

These are the arcana of Edgar Allan Poe: writings on wit, humor, dreams, drunkenness, genius, madness, and apocalypse. Here is the mind of Poe at its most colorful, its most incisive, and its most exceptional.

Edgar Allan Poe's dark, melodic poems and tales of terror and detection are known to readers everywhere, but few are familiar with his cogent literary criticism, or his speculative thinking in science, psychology or philosophy. This book is an attempt to present his lesser known, out of print, or hard to find writings in a single volume, with emphasis on the theoretical and esoteric. The second part, "The French View," includes seminal essays by Poe's famous admirers in France, clarifying his international literary importance.

America has never seen such a personage as Edgar Allan Poe. He is a figure who appears once an epoch, before passing into myth. American critics from Henry James to T. S. Eliot have disparaged and attempted to explain away his influence to no end, save to perpetuate his fame. Even the disdainful Eliot once conceded, "and yet one cannot be sure that one's own writing has *not* been influenced by Poe."

Poe was among the first to attempt a methodological investigation of the unconscious mind. If there was one thing Poe insisted upon, it was *theory*, and his psychological theories (in his *Marginalia*, essays, and reviews) are vital. By focusing on them, we transform those "innocent" tales of mystery and imagination into working blueprints of unconscious mental processes. For what is that magnificent House of Usher, with all of its dark chambers, bizarre furnishings, vaulted ceilings, intricate passages, and its fissure running right up the center, but a pre-Freudian model of the unconscious mind—just as Roderick and Madeline Usher are two halves of a single self. Although he did not scientifically formalize the complex psychopathology of hysteria or perversion, he recorded truths he discerned in his *Marginalia*, notebook jottings which were, for Baudelaire, "the secret chambers of his mind."

> ". . . There is, however, a class of fancies, of exquisite delicacy, which are *not* thoughts, and to which, as yet, I have found it absolutely impossible to adapt language. I use the word *fancies* at random, and merely because I must use *some* word; but the idea commonly attached to the term is not even remotely applicable to

> the shadow of shadows in question. They seem to me rather psychal than intellectual. They arise in the soul (alas, how rarely!) only at its epochs of most intense tranquillity—when bodily and mental health are in perfection—and at those mere points of time where the confines of the waking world blend with those of the world of dreams. I am aware of these "fancies" only when I am upon the brink of sleep, with the consciousness that I am so. I have satisfied myself that this condition exists for an appreciable *point* of time—yet is crowded with these "shadows of shadows"; and for absolute *thought* there is demanded time's endurance . . ."

The importance of this passage from "Between Wakefulness and Sleep," and its date, 1846, is gret indeed. It is a quantum leap in nineteenth century literary consciousness.

Poe chose the gothic tale to explicate obsessive mental states and in that pioneering mode is unsurpassed. Yet he outstrips this genre, for his analytic powers led him to become dissatisfied with gothicizing non-physical forces, and in such atypical and neglected works as "The Imp of the Perverse" and "Between Wakefulness and Sleep" (from the *Marginalia*), Poe makes a bridge to a contemporary psychological treatment of characters and events. As Richard Wilbur observed, Poe is the first writer of the Modernist Age to discover our century's most characteristic subject: the disintegration of personality.

Over half the poems included are from Poe's juvenalia, written between the ages of 18 and 24; they have Romantic sweep, freedom from polished metrics, and reveal much about the youthful prodigy. Many of these poems ("Dreams" 1827, "Imitation" 1827, and "Introduction" 1829-31) were excluded by Poe from the later, standard edition because of their *confessional* nature. Most of the later poems (1835-1849) consist of fragments, drafts, or impromptu verse. There are many gems: "To— —" ("I care not that my earthly lot"), one of his last poems, a reworking of an 1828-29 draft, is a masterpiece of balance, restraint, and solitude.

It is surprising to modern readers that Poe's reputation, in his day, rested not upon the poems or stories (the only immediate success was "The Raven"), but upon his work as a literary critic and editor. Poe found himself ever at odds with his contemporaries. "The fact is," Poe wrote, "some person should write . . . a paper exposing—ruthlessly exposing, the *dessous de cartes* of our literary affairs. He should know how and why it is that the ubiquitous quack in letters can always 'succeed,' while genius (which implies self-respect, with a scorn of creeping and crawling), must inevitably succumb. He should point out the 'easy arts' by which anyone base enough to do it, can get himself placed at the very head of American letters . . ."

With savage dispatch, Poe crushed the literary nonentities of provincial America; with pugilistic audacity (and not always unquestionable mental soundness) he took on the sleeping giant of the North—the bard of *belles lettres* at Harvard, Henry Wadsworth Longfellow. Although the names of those wounded by Poe's critical pen live on only in the dusty, bound volumes of the *Knickerbocker* and *Burton's Gentleman's Magazine*, much of the vitriolic prejudice against Poe which persists today is the result of his ruffling establishment literary feathers. The defamation of Poe's character, from his malicious literary executor Rev. Rufus Griswold to the present, can be traced to the hostility Poe inspired through his articles and reviews. Surely Baudelaire is right that Poe's condemnation by his fellow countrymen springs from a democratic hatred of genius.

Poe devoted his last years to a sprawling philosophical treatise on the nature of the universe. *Eureka: An Essay on the Spiritual and Material Universe* is a brilliant, bizarre, one-hundred-and-fifty-page discourse Poe alternately referred to as an "essay," a "Romance," a "Book of Truths," an "Art-Product," and a "Poem." It is his final effort, his unifying vision, encompassing allegory, metaphor, science fiction, fable, fantasy and the mythopoetic. The sheer bulk of *Eureka* prevents me from including it, but fortunately it is again available, in a Penguin paperback.

Despite the malignity attached to Poe and his works at the time of his death and after, no other American writer has enjoyed such a devoted and scholarly following. In this category is the late Thomas Ollive Mabbott, whose impeccable scholarship I have relied on principally. I am also indebted to the work of Killis Campbell, James K. Harrison, John Carl Miller, John Ward Ostrom, Arthur Hobson Quinn, and Floyd Stovall.

I have made extensive use of the New York Public Library, the Pierpont Morgan Library, the Library of Columbia University, the Huntington Library, and the Doe and Bancroft Libraries of the University of California, Berkeley, and I am grateful to the librarians of these institutions.

I am indebted to my publisher, Lawrence Ferlinghetti, for suggesting the need for such a book and providing refreshing editorial insights, and to my editor, Nancy Joyce Peters, who has overseen the project and taken care in every detail. George Scrivani read the manuscript transcription for accuracy, and Pamela Mosher assisted with design. Lastly, for his critical discernment, judgment, and kind friendship, I should like to thank the poet Philip Lamantia, to whom I dedicate this book.

Raymond Foye
Spring, 1980
North Beach, San Francisco.

Letters

From a letter to John Neal

[Baltimore, Oct.-Nov., 1829]

I am young—not yet twenty—*am* a poet—if deep worship of all beauty can make me *one*—and wish to be so in the common meaning of the word. I would give the world to embody one half the ideas afloat in my imagination. (By the way, do you remember, or did you ever read the exclamation of Shelley about Shakespeare 'What a number of ideas must have been afloat befor [*sic*] such an author could arise!'). I appeal to you as man that loves the same beauty which I adore—the beauty of the natural blue sky and the sunshiny earth—there can be no tie more strong than that of brother for brother—it is not so much that they love one another as that they both love the same parent—their affections are always running in the same direction—the same channel and cannot help mingling. I am and have been from my childhood, an idler. It cannot therefore be said that

'I left a calling for this idle trade
'A duty broke—a father disobeyed—

for I have no father—nor mother.

I am about to publish a volume of "Poems"—the greater part written before I was fifteen. Speaking about 'Heaven', the Editor of the Yankee says, He might write a beautiful, if not a magnificent poem—(the very first words of encouragement I ever remember to have heard). I am very certain that, as yet I have not written *either*—but that I *can*, I will take my oath—if they will give me time.

The poems to be published are 'Al Araaf' [&] 'Tamerlane', one about four, the other about three hundred lines, with smaller pieces. Al Araaf has some good poetry and much extravagance which I have not had time to throw away.

Al Araaf is a tale of another world—the Star discovered by Tycho Brahe, which appeared and disappeared so suddenly—or rather it is no tale at all. I will insert an extract about the palace of its presiding Deity, in which you will see that I have supposed many of the lost sculptures of our world to have flown (in Spirit) to the star Al Araaf—a delicate place more suited to their divinity.

. . .

Edgar A. Poe

From a letter to James Russell Lowell

New-York, July 2. 44.

. . .

I am *not* ambitious—unless negatively. I, now and then feel stirred up to excel a fool, merely because I hate to let a fool imagine that he may excel me. Beyond this I feel nothing of ambition. I really perceive that vanity about which most men merely prate—the vanity of the human or temporal life. I live continually in a reverie of the future. I have no faith in human perfectability. I think that human exertion will have no appreciable effect upon humanity. Man is now only more active—not more happy—nor more wise, than he was 6,000 years ago. The result will never vary—and to suppose that it will, is to suppose that the foregone man has lived in vain—that the foregone time is but the rudiment of the future—that the myriads who have perished have not been upon equal footing with ourselves—nor are we with our posterity. I cannot agree to lose sight of man the individual, in man the mass. —I have no belief in spirituality. I think the word a *mere* word. No one has really a conception of the spirit. We cannot imagine what is not. We deceive ourselves by the idea of infinitely rarefied matter. Matter escapes the senses by degrees—a stone—a metal—a liquid—the atmosphere—a gas—the luminiferous ether. Beyond this there are no other modifications more rare. But to all we attach the notion of a constitution of particles—atomic composition. For this reason only, we think spirit different; for spirit, we say is unparticled, and *therefore* is not matter. But it is clear that if we proceed sufficiently far in our ideas of rarefaction, we shall arrive at a point where the particles coalesce; for, although the particle be infinite, the infinity of littleness in the spaces between them, is an absurdity. —The unparticled matter, permeating & impelling, all things, is God. Its activity is the thought of God—which creates. Man, and other thinking beings, are individualizations of the unparticled matter. Man exists as a "person", by being clothed with matter (the particled matter) which individualizes him. Thus habited, his life is rudimental. What we call "death" is the painful metamorphosis. The stars are the habitations of rudimental beings. But for the necessity of the rudimental life, there would have been no worlds At death, the worm is the butterfly—still material, but of a matter unrecognized by our organs—recognized, occasionally, perhaps, by the sleep-waker, directly—without organs—through the mesmeric medium. Thus a sleep-waker may see ghosts. Divested of the rudimental covering, the being inhabits *space*—what we suppose to be the immaterial universe—passing every where, and acting all things, by mere volition—cognizant of all secrets but that of the nature of God's volition—the motion, or activity, of the unparticled matter.

You speak of an "estimate of my life"—and, from what I have already said, you will see that I have none to give. I have been too deeply conscious of the mutability and evanescence of temporal things, to give any continuous effort to anything—to be consistent in anything. My life has been *whim*—impulse—passion—a longing for solitude—a scorn of all things present, in an earnest desire for the future.

. . .

Believe me your true friend.
E A Poe.

From a letter to Evert A. Duyckinck

Thursday Morning—13th. [Nov. 1845]
85 Amity St. [New York]

My Dear Mr. Duyckinck,

For the first time during two months I find myself entirely myself—dreadfully sick and depressed, but still myself. I seem to have just awakened from some horrible dream, in which all was confusion, and suffering—relieved only by the constant sense of your kindness, and that of one or two other considerate friends. I really believe that I have been mad—but indeed I have had abundant reason to be so. I have made up my mind to a step which will preserve me, for the future, from at least the greater portion of the troubles which have beset me. In the meantime, I have need of the most active exertion to extricate myself from the embarrassments into which I have already fallen—and my object in writing you this note is, (once again) to beg your aid. Of course I need not to say to you that my most urgent trouble is the want of ready money. I find that what I said to you about the prospects of the B.J. [*Broadway Journal*] is strictly correct. The most trifling immediate relief would put it on an excellent footing. All that I want is time in which to look about me; and I think that is your power to afford me this. . . .

Yours
Edgar A Poe.

Letter to Nathaniel P. Willis

[New York] December 30th. 1846

My Dear Willis:—

The paragraph which has been put in circulation respecting my wife's illness, my own, my poverty etc., is now lying before me; together with the beautiful lines by Mrs. Locke and those by Mrs. ——, to which the paragraph has given rise, as well as your kindly and manly comments in "The Home Journal."

The motive of the paragraph I leave to the conscience of him or her who wrote it or suggested it. Since the thing is done, however, and since the concerns of my family are thus pitilessly thrust before the public, I perceive no mode of escape from a public statement of what is true and what erroneous in the report alluded to.

That my wife is ill, then, is true; and you may imagine with what feeling I add that this illness, hopeless from the first, has been heightened and precipitated by her reception, at two different periods, of anonymous letters—one enclosing the paragraph now in question; the other, those published calumnies of Messrs ——, for which I yet hope to find redress in a court of justice.

Of the facts, that I myself have been long and dangerously ill, and that my illness has been a well understood thing among my brethren of the press, the best evidence is afforded by the innumerable paragraphs of personal and literary abuse with which I have been latterly assailed. This matter, however, will remedy itself. At the very first blush of my new prosperity, the gentlemen who toadied me in the old, will recollect themselves and toady me again. You, who know me, will comprehend that I speak of these things only as having served, in a measure, to lighten the gloom of unhappiness, by a gentle and not unpleasant sentiment of mingled pity, merriment and contempt.

That, as the inevitable consequence of so long an illness, I have been in want of money, it would be folly in me to deny—but that I have ever materially suffered from privation, beyond the extent of my capacity for suffering, is not altogether true. That I am "without friends" is a gross calumny, which I am sure *you* never could have believed, and which a thousand noble-hearted men would have good right never to forgive me for permitting to pass unnoticed and undenied. Even in the city of New York I could have no difficulty in naming a hundred persons, to each of whom—when the hour for speaking had arrived—I could and would have applied for aid and with unbounded confidence, and with absolutely *no* sense of humiliation.

I do not think, my dear Willis, that there is any need of my saying more. I am getting better, and may add—if it be any comfort to my enemies—that I have little fear of getting worse. The truth is, I have a great deal to do; and I have made up my mind not to die till it is done.

Sincerely yours,
Edgar A. Poe.

From a letter to George W. Eveleth

New-York—Jan. 4, 1848.

. . .

—You say—"Can you *hint* to me what was the terrible evil" which caused the irregularities so profoundly lamented?" Yes; I can do more than hint. This "evil" was the greatest which can befall a man. Six years ago, a wife, whom I loved as no man ever loved before, ruptured a blood-vessel in singing. Her life was despaired of. I took leave of her forever & underwent all the agonies of her death. She recovered partially and I again hoped. At the end of a year the vessel broke again—I went through precisely the same scene. Again in about a year afterward. Then again—again—again & even once again at varying intervals. Each time I felt all the agonies of her death—and at each accession of the disorder I loved her more dearly & clung to her life with more desperate pertinacity. But I am constitutionally sensitive—nervous in a very unusual degree. I became insane, with long intervals of horrible sanity. During these fits of absolute unconsciousness I drank, God only knows how often or how much. As a matter of course, my enemies referred the insanity to the drink rather than the drink to the insanity. I had indeed, nearly abandoned all hope of a permanent cure when I found one in the *death* of my wife. This I can & do endure as becomes a man—it was the horrible never-ending oscillation between hope & despair which I could *not* longer endure without the total loss of reason. In the death of what was my life, then, I receive a new but—oh God! how melancholy an existence.

. . .

Truly Yours—
E A Poe.

From a letter to George W. Eveleth

New-York—Feb. 29—48.

. . .

—My *habits* are rigorously abstemious and I omit nothing of the natural regimen requisite for health:—i.e,—I rise early, eat moderately, drink nothing but water, and take regular and abundant exercise in the open air. But this is my private life—my studious and literary life—and of course escapes the eye of the world. The desire for society comes upon me only when I have become excited by drink. Then *only* I go—that is, at these times only I *have been* in the practice of going among my friends: who seldom, or in fact never, having seen me unless excited, take it for granted that I am always so. Those who *really* know me, know better. In the meantime I shall turn the general error to account. But enough of this: the causes which maddened me to the drinking point are no more, and I am done drinking, forever.

. . .

I presume you have seen some notices of my late lecture on the Universe. You could have gleaned, however, no idea of what the lecture was, from what the papers said it was. All praised it—as far as I have yet seen—and all absurdly misrepresented it. The only report of it which approaches the truth, is the one I enclose—from the "Express"—written by E. A. Hopkins—a gentleman of much scientific acquirement—son of Bishop Hopkins of Vermont—but he conveys only my general idea, and his digest is full of inaccuracies. I enclose also a slip from the "Courier & Enquirer":—*please return them.* To eke out a chance of your understanding what I really *did* say, I add a loose summary of my propositions & results:

The General Proposition is this: —Because Nothing was, *therefore* All Things are.

1—An inspection of the *universality* of Gravitation—i.e, of the fact that each particle tends, *not* to any one common point, but to *every other* particle—suggests *perfect* totality, or *absolute* unity, as the source of the phenomenon.

2—Gravity is but the mode in which is manifested the tendency of all things to return into their original unity; it is but the reaction of the first Divine Act.

3—The *law* regulating the return—i.e, the *law* of Gravitation—is but a necessary result of the necessary and sole possible mode of equal *irradiation* of matter through space:—this *equable* irradiation is necessary as a basis for the Nebular Theory of Laplace.

4—The Universe of Stars (contradistinguished from the Universe of Space) is limited.

5—Mind is cognizant of Matter *only* through its two properties, attraction and repulsion: a finally consolidated globe of globes, being but *one* particle, would be without attraction, i.e, gravitation; the existence of such a globe presupposes the expulsion of the separative ether which we know to exist between the particles as at present diffused:—thus the final globe would be matter without attraction & repulsion:—but these *are* matter:—then the final globe would be matter without matter: —i.e, no matter at all:—it must disappear. Thus Unity is *Nothingness.*

6—Matter, springing from Unity, sprang from Nothingness:—i.e, was *created.*

7—All will return to Nothingness, in returning to Unity. Read these items *after* the Report. As to the Lecture, I am very quiet about it—but, if you have ever dealt with such topics, you will recognize the novelty & *moment* of my views. What I have propounded will (in good time) revolutionize the world of Physical & Metaphysical Science. I say this calmly—but I say it.

I shall not go till I hear from you.

Truly Yours,
E A Poe

(By the bye, lest you infer that my views, in detail, are the same with those advanced in the *Nebular Hypothesis*, I venture to offer a few addenda, the substance of which was penned, though never printed, several years ago, under the head of—A Prediction. How will *that* do for a postscript?)

Eureka, An Essay on the Spiritual and Material Universe, *delivered as a lecture in New York, Feb. 3, 1848.*

To Sarah Helen Whitman

[New York] Steamboat Nov 14 1848

My own dearest Helen, *so* kind so true, so generous—so unmoved by all that would have moved one who had been less than angel:—beloved of my heart of my imagination of my intellect—life of my life—soul of my soul—dear, dearest Helen, how shall I ever thank you as I ought.

I am calm & tranquil & but for a strange shadow of coming evil which haunts me I should be happy. That I am not supremely happy, even when I feel your dear love at my heart, terrifies me. What can this mean?

Perhaps however it is only the necessary reaction after such terrible excitements.

It is 5 o'clock & the boat is just being made fast to the wharf. I shall start in the train that leaves New York at 7 for Fordham. I write this to show you that I have not *dared* to break my promise to you. And now dear *dearest* Helen be true to me . . .

[Signature missing]

Letter to Maria Clemm

New York [Philadelphia]
July 7. [1849]

My *dear, dear* Mother,—

I have been *so* ill—have had the cholera, or spasms quite as bad, and now can hardly hold the pen [. . .]

The very instant you get this, *come* to me. The joy of seeing you will almost compensate for our sorrows. We can but die together. It is no use to reason with me *now*; I must die. I have no desire to live since I have done "Eureka." I could accomplish nothing more. For your sake it would be sweet to live, but we must die together. You have been all in all to me, darling, ever beloved mother, and dearest, truest friend.

I was never *really* insane, except on occasions where my heart was touched [. . .]

I have been taken to prison once since I came here for getting drunk; but *then* I was not. It was about Virginia.

[No signature]

Edgar Poe—A Reconstructed Portrait

Poems

Preface to Tamerlane and Other Poems

The greater part of the Poems which compose this little volume, were written in the year 1821-2, when the author had not completed his fourteenth year. They were of course not intended for publication; why they are now published concerns no one but himself. Of the smaller pieces very little need be said: they perhaps savor too much of egotism; but they were written by one too young to have any knowledge of the world but from his own breast.

In Tamerlane, he has endeavored to expose the folly of even *risking* the best feelings of the heart at the shrine of Ambition. He is conscious that in this there are many faults, (besides that of the general character of the poem) which he flatters himself he could, with little trouble, have corrected, but unlike many of his predecessors, has been too fond of his early productions to amend them in his *old age*.

He will not say that he is indifferent as to the success of these Poems—it might stimulate him to other attempts—but he can safely assert that failure will not at all influence him in a resolution already adopted. This is challenging criticism—let it be so. *Nos haec novimus esse nihil.**

[*1827*]

* *"I myself know the unimportance of all this." Martial,* Epigrams.

Preface to the Collection of 1845

These trifles are collected and republished chiefly with a view to their redemption from the many improvements to which they have been subjected while going "the rounds of the press." I am naturally anxious that what I have written should circulate as I wrote it, if it circulate at all. In defence of my own taste, nevertheless, it is incumbent on me to say that I think nothing in this volume of much value to the public, or very creditable to myself. Events not to be controlled have prevented me from making, at any time, any serious effort in what, under happier circumstances, would have been the field of my choice. With me poetry has been not a purpose, but a passion; and the passions should be held in reverence; they must not—they cannot at will be excited with an eye to the paltry compensations, or the more paltry commendations, of mankind.

E. A. P.

POETRY
[*Couplet, Age 15*]

Last night, with many cares and toils oppress'd,
Weary, I laid me on a couch to rest—
[*1824*]

TO OCTAVIA

When wit, and wine, and friends have met
And laughter crowns the festive hour
In vain I struggle to forget
Still does my heart confess thy power
And fondly turn to thee!

But Octavia, do not strive to rob
My heart, of all that soothes its pain
The mournful hope that every throb
Will make it break for thee!

[*1827*]

DREAMS

Oh! that my young life were a lasting dream!
My spirit not awak'ning till the beam
Of an Eternity should bring the morrow:
Yes! tho' that long dream were of hopeless sorrow,
'Twere better than the dull reality
Of waking life to him whose heart shall be,
And hath been ever, on the chilly earth,
A chaos of deep passion from his birth!

But should it be—that dream eternally
Continuing—as dreams have been to me
In my young boyhood—should it thus be given,
'Twere folly still to hope for higher Heaven!
For I have revell'd, when the sun was bright
In the summer sky; in dreamy fields of light,
And left unheedingly my very heart
In climes of mine imagining—apart
From mine own home, with beings that have been
Of mine own thought—what more could I have seen?

'Twas once and *only* once and the wild hour
From my remembrance shall not pass—some power
Or spell had bound me—'twas the chilly wind
Came o'er me in the night and left behind
Its image on my spirit, or the moon
Shone on my slumbers in her lofty noon
Too coldly—or the stars—howe'er it was
That dream was as that night wind—let it pass.

I have been happy—tho' but in a dream.
I have been happy—and I love the theme—
Dreams! In their vivid colouring of life—
As in that fleeting, shadowy, misty strife
Of semblance with reality which brings
To the delirious eye more lovely things
Of Paradise and Love—and all our own!
Than young Hope in his sunniest hour hath known.
[*1827-1828*]

Poe walking Highbridge

SPIRITS OF THE DEAD

I

The soul shall find itself alone
'Mid dark thoughts of the gray tomb-stone—
Not one, of all the crowd, to pry
Into thine hour of secrecy:

II

Be silent in that solitude,
    Which is not loneliness—for then
The spirits of the dead who stood
    In life before thee are again
In death around thee—and their will
Shall overshadow thee: be still.

III

The night—tho' clear—shall frown—
And the stars shall look not down,
From their high thrones in the heaven,
With light like Hope to mortals given—
But their red orbs, without beam,
To thy weariness shall seem
As a burning and a fever
Which would cling to thee for ever.

IV

Now are thoughts thou shalt not banish—
Now are visions ne'er to vanish—
From thy spirit shall they pass
No more—like dew-drop from the grass.

V

The breeze—the breath of God—is still—
And the mist upon the hill

Shadowy—shadowy—yet unbroken,
Is a symbol and a token—
How it hangs upon the trees,
A mystery of mysteries!—
[*1827; 1839*]

IMITATION

A dark unfathom'd tide
Of interminable pride—
A mystery, and a dream,
Should my early life seem;
I say that dream was fraught
With a wild, and waking thought
Of beings that have been,
Which my spirit hath not seen,
Had I let them pass me by,
With a dreaming eye!
Let none of earth inherit
That vision of my spirit;
Those thoughts I would control,
As a spell upon his soul:
For that bright hope at last
And that light time have past,
And my worldly rest hath gone
With a sigh as it pass'd on:
I care not tho' it perish
With a thought I then did cherish.
[*1827*]

STANZAS

How often we forget all time, when lone
Admiring Nature's universal throne;
Her words—her wilds—her mountains—the intense
Reply of HERS to OUR intelligence!

I

In youth have I known one with whom the Earth
In secret communing held—as he with it,
In day light, and in beauty from his birth:
Whose fervid, flick'ring torch of life was lit
From the sun and stars, when he had drawn forth
A passionate light—such for his spirit was fit—
And yet that spirit knew not—in the hour
Of its own fervor—what had o'er it power.

2

Perhaps it may be that my mind is wrought
To a fervor by the moon beam that hangs o'er.
But I will half believe that wild light fraught
With more of sov'reignty than ancient lore
Hath ever told—or is it of a thought
The unembodied essence, and no more
That with a quick'ning spell doth o'er us pass
As dew of the night-time, o'er the summer grass?

3

Doth o'er us pass, when, as th' expanding eye
To the lov'd object—so the tear to the lid
Will start, which lately slept in apathy?
And yet it need not be—(that object) hid
From us in life—but common—which doth lie
Each hour before us—but *then* only bid
With a strange sound, as of a harp-string broken
T' awake us—'Tis a symbol and a token.

4

Of what in other worlds shall be—and giv'n
In beauty by our God, to those alone
Who otherwise would fall from life and Heav'n
Drawn by their heart's passion, and that tone,
That high tone of the spirit which hath striv'n
Tho' not with Faith—with godliness—whose throne
With desp'rate energy 't hath beaten down;
Wearing its own deep feeling as a crown.
[*1827*]

TO— —

1

Should my early life seem,
(As well it might,) a dream—
Yet I build no faith upon
The king Napoleon—
I look not up afar
For my destiny in a star:

2

In parting from you now
Thus much I will avow—
There are beings, and have been
Whom my spirit had not seen
Had I let them pass me by
With a dreaming eye—
If my peace hath fled away
In a night—or in a day—
In a vision—or in none—
Is it therefore the less gone?—

3

I am standing 'mid the roar
Of a weather-beaten shore,
And I hold with my hand
Some particles of sand—
How few! and how they creep
Thro' my fingers to the deep!
My early hopes? no—they
Went gloriously away,
Like lightning from the sky
At once—and so will I.

4

So young? ah! no—not now—
Thou hast not seen my brow,
But they tell thee I am proud—
They lie—they lie aloud—
My bosom beats with shame
At the paltriness of name
With which they dare combine
A feeling such as mine—
Nor Stoic? I am not:
In the terror of my lot
I laugh to think how poor
That pleasure "to endure!"
What! shade of Zeno!—I!
Endure!—no—no—defy.
[*1829*]

TO— —

I

The bowers whereat, in dreams, I see
   The wantonest singing birds
Are lips—and all thy melody
   Of lip-begotten words—

2

Thine eyes, in Heaven of heart enshrin'd
   Then desolately fall,
O! God! on my funereal mind
   Like starlight on a pall—

3

Thy heart—*thy* heart!—I wake and sigh,
   And sleep to dream till day
Of the truth that gold can never buy—
   Of the trifles that it may.
[*1829*]

INTRODUCTION

Romance, who loves to nod and sing,
With drowsy head and folded wing,
Among the green leaves as they shake
Far down within some shadowy lake,
To me a painted paroquet
Hath been—a most familiar bird—
Taught me my alphabet to say—
To lisp my very earliest word
While in the wild-wood I did lie

A child—with a most knowing eye.
Succeeding years, too wild for song,
Then roll'd like tropic storms along,
Where, tho' the garish lights that fly
Dying along the troubled sky,
Lay bare, thro' vistas thunder-riven,
The blackness of the general Heaven,
That very blackness yet doth fling
Light on the lightning's silver wing.

For, being an idle boy lang syne,
Who read Anacreon rhymes
Were almost passionate sometimes—
And by strange alchemy of brain
His pleasures always turn'd to pain—
His naivete to wild desire—
His wit to love—his wine to fire—
And so, being young and dipt in folly
I fell in love with melancholy,
And used to throw my earthly rest
And quiet all away in jest—
I could not love except where Death
Was mingling his with Beauty's breath—
Or Hymen, Time, and Destiny
Were stalking between her and me.

O, then the eternal Condor years
So shook the very Heavens on high,
With tumult as they thunder'd by;
I had no time for idle cares,
Thro' gazing on the unquiet sky!
Or if an hour with calmer wing
Its down did on my spirit fling,
That little hour with lyre and rhyme
To while away—forbidden thing!
My heart half fear'd to be a crime
Unless it trembled with the string.

But *now* my soul has too much room—
Gone are the glory and the gloom—

The black hath mellow'd into grey,
And all the fires are fading away.

My draught of passion hath been deep—
I revell'd, and I now would sleep—
And after-drunkenness of soul
Succeeds the glories of the bowl—
An idle longing night and day
To dream my very life away.

But dreams—of those who dream as I,
Aspiringly, are damned, and die:
Yet should I swear I mean alone,
By notes so very shrilly blown,
To break upon Time's monotone,
While yet my vapid joy and grief
Are tintless of the yellow leaf—
Why not an imp the greybeard hath,
Will shake his shadow in my path—
And even the greybeard will o'erlook
Connivingly my dreaming-book.
[*1829-1831*]

MYSTERIOUS STAR!

Mysterious star!
Thou wert my dream
All a long summer night—
Be now my theme!
By this clear stream,
Of thee will I write;
Meantime from afar
Bathe me in light!

Thy world has not the dross of ours,
Yet all the beauty—all the flowers

That list our love, or deck our bowers
In dreamy gardens, where do lie
Dreamy maidens all the day,
While the silver winds of Circassy
On violet couches faint away.

Little—oh! little dwells in thee
Like unto what on earth we see:
Beauty's eye is here the bluest
In the falsest and untruest—
On the sweetest air doth float
The most sad and solemn note—
If with thee be broken hearts,
Joy so peacefully departs,
That its echo still doth dwell,
Like the murmur in the shell.
Thou! thy framing is so holy
Sorrow is not melancholy.
[*1831*]

TO— —

Sleep on, sleep on, another hour—
   I would not break so calm a sleep,
To wake to sunshine and to show'r,
   To smile and weep.

Sleep on, sleep on, like sculptured thing,
   Majestic, beautiful art thou;
Sure seraph fans thee with his wing
   And fans thy brow—

We would not deem thee child of earth,
   For, O, angelic is thy form!
But that in heav'n thou had'st thy birth,
   Where comes no storm.

To mar the bright, the perfect flow'r,
  But all is beautiful and still—
And the golden sands proclaim the hour
  Which brings no ill.

Sleep on, sleep on, some fairy dream
  Perchance is woven in thy sleep—
But, O, thy spirit, calm, serene,
  Must wake to weep.
[*1833*]

DACTYLIC COUPLET

Can it be fancied that Deity ever vindictively
Made in his image a manikin merely to madden it?
[*1846*]

DEEP IN EARTH

Deep in earth my love is lying
  And I must weep alone.
[*1847*]

TO LOUISE OLIVER HUNTER

Though I turn, I fly not—
  I cannot depart;
I would try, but try not
  To release my heart.
And my hopes are dying
While, on dreams relying,
  I am spelled by art.

Thus the bright snake coiling
  Neath the forest tree
Wins the bird, beguiling
  To come down and see:
Like that bird the lover
Round his fate will hover
Till the blow is over
  And he sinks—like me.
February 14, 1847

LINES ON ALE

Fill with mingled cream and amber,
  I will drain that glass again.
Such hilarious visions clamber
  Through the chamber of my brain—
Quaintest thoughts—queerest fancies
  Come to life and fade away;
What care I how time advances?
  I am drinking ale today.
[*1848*]

(Thought to have been written at Washington Tavern in Lowell, Massachusetts, where it hung on the saloon wall until about 1920.)

TO– –

I heed not that my earthly lot
   Hath—little of earth in it—
That years of love have been forgot
   In the hatred of a minute:—
I mourn not that the desolate
   Are happier, sweet, than I,
But that *you* sorrow for *my* fate
   Who am a passer by.
[*1828; 1849*]

from the Marginalia

WHEN MUSIC AFFECTS US TO TEARS

When music affects us to tears, seemingly causeless, we weep *not*, as Gravina supposes, from "excess of pleasure"; but through excess of an impatient, petulant sorrow that, as mere mortals, we are as yet in no condition to banquet upon those supernal ecstasies of which the music merely affords us a suggestive and indefinite glimpse.

THE QUEST OF REASON

The theorizers on Government, who pretend always to "begin with the beginning," commence with Man in what they call his *natural* state—the savage. What right have they to suppose this his natural state? Man's chief idiosyncrasy being reason, it follows that his savage condition—his condition of action *without* reason—is his *un*natural state. The more he reasons, the nearer he approaches the position to which this chief idiosyncrasy irresistibly impels him; and not until he attains this position with exactitude—not until his reason has exhausted itself for his improvement—not until he has stepped upon the highest pinnacle of civilization—will his *natural* state be ultimately reached, or thoroughly determined.

THE UNIVERSE IS A PLOT OF GOD

The pleasure which we derive from any exertion of human ingenuity is in the direct ratio of the *approach* to this species of reciprocity between cause and effect. In the construction of *plot*, for example, in fictitious literature, we should aim at so arranging the points, or incidents, that we cannot distinctly see, in respect to any one of them, whether that one depends from any other, or upholds it. In this sense, of course, perfection of plot is unattainable *in fact*,—because Man is the constructor. The plots of God are perfect. The Universe is a Plot of God.

SIGHT & SOUND

"The right angle of light's incidence produces a sound upon one of the Egyptian pyramids." This assertion, thus expressed, I have encountered somewhere—probably in one of those Notes to Appollonius. It is nonsense, I suppose,—but it will not do to speak hastily. The orange ray of the spectrum and the buzz of the gnat (which never rises above the second A), affect me with nearly similar sensations. In hearing the gnat, I perceive the color. In perceiving the color, I seem to hear the gnat.

Here the vibrations of the tympanum caused by the wings of the fly, may, from within, induce abnormal vibration of the retina, similar to those which the orange ray induces, normally, from without. By *similar*, I do not mean of equal rapidity—this would be folly;—but each millionth undulation, for example, of the retina, might accord with one of the tympanum; and I doubt whether this would not be sufficient for the effect.

RE-LIVING THE LIFE

"That evil predominates over good, becomes evident, when we consider that there can be found no aged person who would be willing to re-live the life he has already lived."—Volney.

The idea here, is not distinctly made out; for unless through the context, we cannot be sure whether the author means merely this:—that every aged person fancies he might, in a different course of life, have been happier than in the one actually lived, and, for this reason, would not be willing to live *his* life over again, *but some other life*;—or, whether the sentiment intended is this:—that if, upon the grave's brink, the choice were offered any aged person between the expected death and the re-living the old life, that person would prefer to die.

The first proposition is, perhaps, true; but the last (which is the one designed) is not only doubtful, in point of mere fact, but is of no effect, even if granted to be true, in sustaining the original proposition—that evil predominates over good.

It is assumed that the aged person will not re-live his life, because he *knows* that its evil predominated over its good. The source of error lies in the word "knows"—in the assumption that we can ever be, really, in possession of the whole knowledge to which allusion is cloudily made. But there is a *seeming*—a fictitious knowledge; and this very seeming knowledge it is, of what the life has been, which incapacitates the aged person from deciding the question upon its merits. He blindly deduces a notion of the happiness of the original real life—a notion of its preponderating evil or good—from a consideration of the secondary or supposititious one. In his estimate he merely strikes a balance between *events*, and leaves quite out of the account the elastic *Hope* which is the Harbinger and the Eos of all. Man's real life is happy, chiefly because he is ever expecting that it will soon be so. But, in regarding the supposititious life, we paint to ourselves chill certainties for warm expectations, and grievances quadrupled in being foreseen. But because we cannot avoid doing this—strain our imaginative faculties as we will—because it is so very difficult—so nearly impossible a task, to fancy the known unknown—the done accomplished—and because (through our inability to fancy all this) we prefer death to a secondary life—does it, in any manner, follow that the evil of the properly-considered real existence *does* predominate over the good?

In order that a just estimate be made by Mr. Volney's "aged person," and from this estimate a judicious choice:—in order, again, that from this estimate and choice, we deduce any clear comparison of good with evil in human existence, it will be necessary that we obtain the opinion, or "choice," upon this point, from an aged person, who shall be in position to appreciate, with precision, the hopes he is naturally led to leave out of question, but which reason tells us he would as strongly experience as ever, in the absolute re-living of the life. On the other hand, too, he must be in condition to dismiss from the estimate the fears which he actually feels, and which show him bodily the ills that are to happen, but which fears, again, reason assures us, he would *not*, in the absolute secondary life, encounter. Now what mortal was ever in condition to make these allowances?—to perform impossibilities in giving these considerations their due weight? What mortal, then, was ever in condition to make a well-grounded choice? How, from an ill-grounded one, are we to make deductions which shall guide us aright? How out of error shall we fabricate truth?

A GENUS IRRITABILE

That poets (using the word comprehensively, as including artists in general) are a *genus irritabile*, is well understood; but the *why*, seems not to be commonly seen. An artist *is* an artist only by dint of his exquisite sense of Beauty—a sense affording him rapturous enjoyment, but at the same time implying, or involving, an equally exquisite sense of Deformity or disproportion. Thus a wrong—an injustice—done a poet who is really a poet, excites him to a degree which, to ordinary apprehension, appears disproportionate with the wrong. Poets *see* injustice—*never* where it does not exist—but very often where the unpoetical see no injustice whatever. Thus the poetic irritability has no reference to "temper" in the vulgar sense, but merely to a more than usual clear-sightedness in respect to Wrong:—this clear-sightedness being nothing more than a corollary from the vivid perception of Right—of justice—of proportion, in a word, of το καλον. But one thing is clear—that the man who is *not* "irritable," (to the ordinary apprehension,) is *no poet.*

"GREAT WIT TO MADNESS IS NEARLY ALLIED . . ."

Let a man succeed ever so evidently—ever so demonstrably—in

many different displays of *genius*, the envy of criticism will agree with the popular voice in denying him more than *talent*, in any. Thus a poet who has achieved a great (by which I mean an effective) poem, should be cautious not to distinguish himself in any other walk of Letters. In especial—let him make no effort in Science—unless anonymously, or with the view of waiting patiently the judgement of posterity. Because universal or even versatile geniuses have rarely or never been known, *therefore*, thinks the world, none such can ever be. A "therefore" of this kind is, with the world, conclusive. But what is the *fact*, as taught us by analysis of mental powers? Simply, the *highest* genius—that the genius which all men instantaneously acknowledge as such—which acts upon individuals, as well as upon the mass, by a species of magnetism incomprehensible but irresistible and *never resisted*—that this genius which demonstrates itself in the simplest gesture—or even by the absence of all—this genius which speaks without a voice and flashes from the unopened eye—is but the result of generally large mental power existing in a state of *absolute proportion*—so that no one faculty has undue predominance. *That* factitious "genius"—that "genius" in the popular sense—which is but the manifestation of the abnormal predominance of some one faculty over all the others—and, of course, at the expense and to the detriment, of all the others—is a result of mental disease or rather, of organic malformation of mind:—it is this and nothing more. Not only will such "genius" fail, if turned aside from the path indicated by its predominant faculty; but, even when pursuing this path—when producing those works in which, certainly, it is *best* calculated to succeed—will give unmistakeable indications of *unsoundness*, in respect to general intellect. Hence, indeed, arises the just idea that

"Great wit to madness nearly is allied."

I say "*just* idea;" for by "great wit," in this case, the poet intends precisely the pseudo-genius to which I refer. The true genius, on the other hand, is necessarily, if not universal in its manifestations, at least capable of universality; and if, attempting all things, it succeeds in one rather better than another, this is merely on account of a certain bias by which *Taste* leads it with more earnestness in the one direction than in the other. With equal zeal, it would succeed equally in all.

To sum up our results in respect to this very simple, but much *vexata quaestio*:—

What the world calls "genius" is the state of mental disease arising from the undue predominance of some one of the faculties. The works of such genius are never sound in themselves and, in especial, always betray the general mental insanity.

The proportion of the mental faculties, in a case where the general mental power is *not* inordinate, gives that result which we distinguish as *talent*:—and the talent is greater or less, first, as the general mental power is greater or less; and, secondly, as the proportion of the faculties is more or less absolute.

The proportion of the faculties, in a case where the mental power is inordinately great, gives that result which *is* the true *genius* (but which, on account of the proportion and seeming simplicity of its works, is seldom acknowledged to *be* so;) and the genius is greater or less, first, as the general mental power is more or less inordinately great; and, secondly, as the proportion of the faculties is more or less absolute.

An objection will be made:—that the greatest excess of mental power, however proportionate, does not seem to satisfy our idea of genius, unless we have, in addition, sensibility, passion, energy. The reply is, that the "absolute proportion" spoken of, when applied to inordinate mental power, gives, as a result, the appreciation of Beauty and a horror of Deformity which we call sensibility, together with that intense vitality, which is implied when we speak of "Energy" or "Passion."

THE FLIGHT OF THE SPIRIT

In the life of every man there occurs at least one epoch when the spirit seems to abandon, for a brief period, the body, and, elevating itself above mortal affairs just so far as to get a comprehensive and *general* view, makes thus an estimate of its humanity, as accurate as is possible, under any circumstances, to that particular spirit. The soul here separates itself from its own idiosyncrasy, or individuality, and considers its own being, not as apertaining solely to itself, but as a portion of the universal Ens. All the important good resolutions which we keep—all startling, marked regenerations of character—are brought about at these *crises* of life. And thus it is our *sense of self* which debases, and which keeps us debased.

DREAM AND REVERIE

We may judge the degree of abstraction in one who meditates, by the manner in which he receives an interruption. If he is much startled, his reverie was not profound; and the converse. Thus the affectation of the tribe of pretended mental-absentees, becomes transparent. These people awake from their musings with a start, and an air of bewilderment, as men naturally awake from dreams that have a close semblance of reality. But they are, clearly, ignorant that the phenomena of dreaming differ, radically, from those of reverie—of which latter the mesmeric condition is the extreme.

ON THE IMAGINATION

That the imagination has not been unjustly ranked as supreme among the mental faculties, appears from the intense consciousness, on the part of the imaginative man, that the faculty in question brings his soul often to a glimpse of things supernal and eternal—to the very verge of the *great secrets*. There are moments, indeed, in which he perceives the faint perfumes, and hears the melodies of a happier world. Some of the most profound knowledge—perhaps all *very* profound knowledge—has originated from a highly stimulated imagination. Great intellects *guess* well. The laws of Kepler were, professedly, *guesses*.

INTUITIVE PERCEPTIONS

The intuitive and seemingly casual perception by which we often attain knowledge, when reason herself falters and abandons the effort, appears to resemble the sudden glancing at a star, by which we see it more clearly than by a direct gaze; or the half closing the eyes in looking at a plot of grass the more fully to appreciate the intensity of its green.

A STRUGGLE OF THE SOUL

There are few men of that peculiar sensibility which is at the root of genius, who, in early youth, have not expended much of their mental energy in *living too fast*; and, in later years, comes the unconquerable desire to goad the imagination up to that point which it would have attained in an ordinary, normal, or well-regulated life. The earnest longing for artificial excitement, which, unhappily, has characterized too many eminent men, may thus be regarded as a psychal want, or necessity,—an effort to regain the lost,—a struggle of the soul to assume the position which, under other circumstances, would have been its due.

MEN OF GENIUS . . .

Men of genius are far more abundant than is supposed. In fact, to appreciate thoroughly the work of what we call genius, is to possess all the genius by which the work was produced. But the person appreciating may be utterly incompetent to reproduce the work, or any thing similar, and this solely through lack of what may be termed the constructive ability—a matter quite independent of what we agree to understand in the term "genius" itself. This ability is based, to be sure, in great part, upon the faculty of analysis, enabling the artist to get full view of the machinery of his proposed effect, and thus work it and regulate it at will; but a great deal depends also upon properties strictly moral—for example, upon patience, upon concentrativeness or the power of holding the attention steadily to the one purpose, upon self-dependence and contempt for all opinion which is opinion and no more—in especial, upon energy or industry. So vitally important is this last, that it may well be doubted if any thing to which we have been accustomed to give the title of "a work of genius" are few, while mere men of genius are, as I say, abundant. The Romans, who excelled us in acuteness of *observation*, while falling below us in induction from facts observed, seem to have been so fully aware of the inseparable connection between industry and a "work of genius" as to have adopted the error that industry, in great measure, was genius itself. The highest compliment is intended by a Roman when, of an epic, or any thing similar, he says that it is written *industria mirabili* or *incredibili industria*.

ON MESMERIC REVELATION

The Swedenborgians inform me that they have discovered all that I said in a magazine article, entitled "Mesmeric Revelation," to be absolutely true, although at first they were very strongly inclined to doubt my veracity—a thing which, in that particular instance, I never dreamed of not doubting myself. The story is a pure fiction from begining to end.

BETWEEN WAKEFULNESS AND SLEEP

Some Frenchman—possibly Montaigne—says: "People talk about thinking, but for my part I never think, except when I sit down to write." It is this never thinking, unless when we sit down to write, which is the cause of so much indifferent composition. But perhaps there is something more involved in the Frenchman's observation than meets the eye. It is certain that the mere act of inditing, tends, in a great degree, to the logicalization of thought. Whenever, on account of its vagueness, I am dissatisfied with a conception of the brain, I resort forthwith to the pen, for the purpose of obtaining, through its aid, the necessary form, consequence, and precision.

How very commonly we hear it remarked, that such and such thoughts are beyond the compass of words! I do not believe that any thought, properly so called, is out of the reach of language. I fancy, rather that where difficulty of expression is experienced, there is, in the intellect which experiences it, a want either of deliberateness or method. For my own part, I have never had a thought which I could not set down in words, with even more distinctness than that with which I conceived it:—as I have observed, the thought is logicalized by the effort at (written) expression. There is, however, a class of fancies, of exquisite delicacy, which are *not* thoughts, and to which, *as yet*, I have found it absolutely impossible to adapt language. I use the word *fancies* at random, and merely because I must use *some* word; but the idea commonly attached to the term is not even remotely applicable to the shadows of shadows in question. They seem to me rather psychal than intellectual. They arise in the soul (alas, how rarely!) only at its epochs of most intense tranquility—when the bodily and mental health are in perfection—and at those mere points of time where the confines of the waking world blend with those of the world of dreams. I am aware of these "fancies" only when I am upon the very brink of sleep, with the consciousness that I am so. I have satisfied myself that this condition exists but for an inappreciable *point* of time—yet it is crowded with these "shadows of shadows"; and for absolute *thought* there is demanded time's *endurance*.

These "fancies" have in them a pleasurable ecstasy, as far beyond the most pleasurable of the world of wakefulness, or of dreams, as the Heaven of the Northman theology is beyond its Hell. I regard the visions, even as they arise, with an awe which, in some measure, moderates or tranquillizes the ecstasy—I so regard them, through a conviction (which seems a portion of the ecstasy itself) that this ecstasy, in itself, is of a character supernal to the Human Nature—is a glimpse of the spirit's outer world; and I arrive at this conclusion—if this term is at all applicable to instantaneous intuition by a perception that the delight experienced has, as its element, but *the absoluteness of novelty*. I say the absoluteness—for in these fancies—let me now term them psychal impressions—there is really nothing even approximate in character to impressions ordinarily received. It is as if the five senses were supplanted by five myriad others alien to mortality.

Now, so entire is my faith in the *power of words*, that, at times, I have believed it impossible to embody the evanescence of fancies such as I have attempted to describe. In experiments with this end in view, I have proceeded so far as, first, to control (when the bodily and mental health are good) the existence of the condition:—that is to say, I can now (unless when ill) be sure that the condition will supervene, if I so wish it, at the point of time already described:—of its supervention, until lately, I could never be certain, even under the most favorable circumstances. I mean to say, merely, that now I can be sure, when all circumstances are favorable, of the supervention of the condition, and feel even the capacity of inducing or compelling it:—the favorable circumstances, however, are not the less rare—else I had compelled, already, the Heaven into the Earth.

I have proceeded so far, secondly, as to prevent the lapse from *the point* of which I speak—the point of blending between wakefulness and sleep—as to prevent at will, I say, the lapse from this border-ground into the dominion of sleep. Not that I can *continue* the condition—not that I can render the point more than a point—but that I can startle myself from the point into wakefulness; *and thus transfer the point itself into the realm of Memory*; convey its impressions, or more properly their recollections, to a situation where (although still for a very brief period) I can survey them with the eye of analysis.

For these reasons—that is to say, because I have been enabled to accomplish thus much—I do not altogether despair of embodying in words at least enough of the fancies in question to convey, to certain classes of intellect, a shadowy conception of their character.

In saying this I am not to be understood as supposing that the fancies, or psychal impressions, to which I allude, are confined to my individual self—are not, in a word, common to all mankind—for on this point it is quite impossible that I should form an opinion—but nothing can be more certain than even a partial record of the impressions would startle the universal intellect of mankind, by the *supremeness of the novelty* of the material employed, and of its consequent suggestions. In a word—should I ever write a paper on this topic, the world would be compelled to acknowledge that, at last, I have done an original thing.

FIRST IMPRESSIONS

In general, our first impressions are true ones—the chief difficulty is in making sure which *are* the first. In early youth we read a poem, for instance, and are enraptured with it. At manhood we are assured by our reason that we had no reason to be enraptured. But some years elapse, and we return to our primitive admiration, just as a matured judgement enables us precisely to see what and why we admired.

Thus, as individuals, we think in cycles, and may, from the frequency or infrequency of our revolutions about the various thought-centres, form an accurate estimate of the advance of our thought toward maturity. It is really wonderful to observe how closely, in all the essentials of truth, the child-opinion coincides with that of the man proper—of the man at his best.

And as with individuals so, perhaps, with mankind. When the world begins to return, frequently, to its first impressions, we shall then be warranted in looking for the millennium—or whatever it is: we may safely take it for granted that we are attaining our maximum of wit, and of the happiness which is thence to ensue. The indications of such a return are, at the present, like the visits of angels—but we have them now and then—in the case, for example, of *credulity*. The philosophic, of late days, are distinguished by that very facility in belief which was the characteristic of the illiterate half a century ago. Skepticism in regard to apparent miracles, is not, as formerly, an evidence either of superior wisdom or knowledge. In a word, the wise now believe—yesterday they would not believe—and the day before yesterday (in the time of Strabo, for example) they believed, exclusively, anything and everything: here, then, is one of the indicative cycles completed—indicative of the world's approach to years of discretion. I mentioned Strabo merely as an exception to the rule of his epoch—(just as one in a hurry for an illustration, might describe Mr. So and So to be witty or amiable as Mr. This and That is *not*—for so rarely did men reject in Strabo's time, and so much more rarely did they *err* by rejection, that the skepticism of this philosopher must be regarded as one of the most remarkable anomalies on record.

Poe at work under the eye of his cat, Catalina, who would perch on his shoulder as he wrote

THE DRUGGING SYSTEM IN MEDICAL PRACTICE

The drugging system, in medical practice, seems to me to be a modification of the idea of *penance*, which has haunted the world since its infancy—the idea that the voluntary endurance of pain is atonement for sin. In this, the primary phase of folly, there is at least a show of rationality. Man offends the Deity; thus appears to arise a necessity for retribution, or more strictly, a desire, on the part of Deity, to punish. The *self*-infliction of punishment, then, seemed to include at once an acknowledgement of error, zeal in anticipating the will of God, and expiation of the wrong. The thought, thus stated, however absurd, is not unnatural; but the principle being gradually left out of sight, mankind at length found itself possessed of the naked idea that in general, the suffering of mankind is grateful to the Creator:—hence the Dervishes, the Simeons, the monastic hair-cloths and shoe-peas, the present Puritanism and cant about the "mortification of the flesh." From this point the conceit makes another lapse; the fancy took root, that *in the voluntary endurance of ill there existed in the abstract a tendency to good*; and it was but in pursuance of this fancy that, in sickness, remedies were selected in the ratio of their repulsiveness. How else shall we account for the fact, that in ninety-nine cases out of a hundred, the articles of Materia Medica are distasteful?

THE ADOPTION OF A NAME FOR OUR COUNTRY

It is a thousand pities that the puny witticisms of a few professional objectors should have power to prevent, even for a year, the adoption of a name for our country. At present we have, clearly none. There should be no hesitation about "Appalachia." In the first place, it is distinctive. "America" is not, and can never be made so. *We* may legislate as much as we please, and assume for our country whatever name we think right—but to us it will be no name, to any purpose for which a name is needed, unless we can take it away from the regions which employ it at present. South America is "America," and will insist upon remaining so. In the second place, "Appalachia" is indigenous, springing from one of the most magnificent and distinctive features of the country itself. Thirdly, in employing this word we do honor to the Aborigines, whom, hitherto, we have at all points unmercifully despoiled, assassinated, and dishonored. Fourthly, the name is the suggestion of, perhaps, the most deservedly eminent among all pioneers of American literature. It is but just that Mr. Irving should name the land for which, in letters, he first established a name. The last, and by far the most truly important consideration of all, however, is the music of "Appalachia" itself; nothing could be more sonorous, more liquid, or of fuller volume, while its length is just sufficient for dignity. How the gutteral "Alleghania" could ever have been preferred for a moment is difficult to conceive. I yet hope to find "Appalachia" assumed.

THE NATURE OF GENIUS

The more there are great excellences in a work, the less I am surprised at finding great demerits. When a book is said to have many faults, nothing is decided, and I cannot tell, by this, whether it is excellent or execrable. It is said of another that it is without fault; if the account be just, the work cannot *be excellent. —Trublet.*

The "cannot" here is much too positive. The opinions of Trublet are wonderfully prevalent, but they are none the less demonstrably false. It is merely the *indolence* of genius which has given them currency. The truth seems to be that genius of the highest order lives in a state of perpetual vacillation between ambition and *the scorn of it*. The ambition of a great intellect is at best negative. It struggles—it labors—it creates—not because excellence is desirable, but because to be excelled where there exists a sense of the power excel, is unendurable. Indeed I cannot help thinking that the *greatest* intellects (since these most clearly perceive the laughable absurdity of human ambition) remain contentedly "mute and inglorious." At all events, the *vacillation* of which I speak is the prominent feature of genius. Alternately inspired and depressed, its inequalities of mood are stamped upon its labors. This is the truth, generally—but it is a truth very different from the assertion involved in the "cannot" of Trublet. Give to genius a sufficiently enduring *motive*, and the result will be harmony, proportion, beauty, perfection—all, in this case, synonymous terms. Its supposed "inevitable" irregularities shall not be found:—for it is clear that the susceptibility to impressions of beauty—that susceptibility which is the most important element of genius—implies an equally exquisite sensitiveness and aversion to deformity. The motive—the *enduring* motive—has indeed, hitherto, fallen *rarely* to the lot of genius, but I could point to several compositions which, "without any fault," are yet "excellent"—supremely so. The world, too, is on the threshold of an epoch, wherein, with the aid of a calm philosophy, such compositions shall be ordinarily the work of that genius which is *true*. One of the first and most essential steps, in overpassing this threshold, will serve to kick out of the world's way this very idea of Trublet—this untenable and paradoxical idea of the incompatibility of genius with *art*.

MY HEART LAID BARE

If any ambitious man have a fancy to revolutionize, at one effort, the universal world of human thought, human opinion, and human sentiment, the opportunity is his own—the road to immortal renown lies straight, open, and unencumbered before him. All he has to do is to write and publish a very little book. Its title should be simple—a few plain words—"My Heart Laid Bare." But—this little book must be *true to its title.*

Now, it is not very singular that, with the rabid thirst for notoriety which distinguishes so many of mankind—so many, too, who care not a fig what is thought of them after death, there should not be found one man having sufficient hardihood to write this little book? To *write*, I say. There are ten thousand men who, if the book were once written, would laugh at the notion of being disturbed by its publication during their life, and who could not even conceive *why* they should object to its being published after their death. But to write it—*there* is the rub. No man dare write it. No man ever will dare write it. No man *could* write it, even if he dared. The paper would shrivel and blaze at every touch of the fiery pen.

ON THE TOPICS OF GOD & THE SOUL

After reading all that has been written, and after thinking all that can be thought, on the topics of God and the soul, the man who has a right to say that he thinks at all, will find himself face to face with the conclusion that, on these topics, the most profound thought is that which can be the least easily distinguished from the most superficial sentiment.

THE PURE IMAGINATION

The *pure Imagination* chooses, from *either Beauty or Deformity*, only the most combinable things hitherto uncombined; the compound, as a general rule, partaking, in character, of beauty, or sublimity, in the ratio of the respective beauty or sublimity of the things combined—which are themselves still to be considered as atomic—that is to say, as previous combinations. But, as often analogously happens in physical chemistry, so not unfrequently does it occur in the chemistry of the intellect, that the admixture of the two elements results in a something that has nothing of the qualities of either. . . . Thus, the range of Imagination is unlimited. Its materials extend throughout the universe. Even out of deformities it fabricates that *Beauty* which is at once its sole object and its inevitable test. But, in general, the richness or force of the matters combined; the facility of discovering combinable novelties worth combining; and, especially, the absolute "chemical combination" of the completed mass—are the particulars to be regarded in our estimate of Imagination. It is this thorough harmony of an imaginative work which so often causes it to be undervalued by the thoughtless, through the character of *obviousness* which is superinduced. We are apt to find ourselves asking *why* these combinations have never been imagined before.

OUR PRESENT EXISTENCE

It is by no means an irrational fancy that, in a future existence, we shall look upon what we think our present existence, as a dream.

VILLAINY AND VIRTUE

In looking at the world *as it is*, we shall find it folly to deny that, to worldly success, a surer path is Villainy than Virtue. What the Scriptures mean by the "*leaven* of unrighteousness" is that leaven by which men *rise.*

TO BE THOROUGHLY CONVERSANT WITH MAN'S HEART . . .

"A little learning," in the sense intended by the poet, *is*, beyond all question, "a dangerous thing":—but, in regard to *that* learning which we call "knowledge of the world," it is *only* a little that is *not* dangerous. To be thoroughly conversant with Man's heart, is to take our final lesson in the iron-clasped volume of Despair.

HARMONY AND PROPORTION IN ART

The phrase of which our poets, and more especially our orators, are so fond—the phrase "music of the spheres"—has arisen simply from a misconception of the Platonic word μουσκη—which, with the Athenians, included not merely the harmonies of tune and time, but *proportion* generally. In recommending the study of "music" as "the best education for the soul," Plato referred to the cultivation of the Taste, in contradistinction from that of Pure Reason. By the "music of the spheres" is meant the agreements—the adaptations—in a word, the proportions—developed in the astronomical laws. He had *no* allusion to music in *our* understanding of the term. The word "mosaic," which we derive from μουσκη, refers, in like manner, to the proportion, or harmony of color, observed—or which should be observed—in the department of Art so entitled.

THE VEIL OF THE SOUL

Were I called on to define, *very* briefly, the term "Art," I should call it "the reproduction of what the Senses perceive in Nature through the veil of the soul." The mere imitation, however accurate, of what *is* in Nature, entitles no man to the sacred name of "Artist." Denner* was no artist. The grapes of Zeuxis were *in*artistic—unless in a bird's eye view; and not even the curtain of Parrhasius could conceal his deficiency in point of genius. I have mentioned "the *veil* of the soul." Something of the kind appears indispensable in Art. We can, at any time, double the true beauty of an actual landscape by half closing our eyes as we look at it. The naked Senses sometimes see too little—but then *always* they see too much.

* *Balthsam Denner, 1685-1749, German painter.*

THE ACCURSED INTELLECT

I have sometimes amused myself by endeavoring to fancy what would be the fate of an individual gifted, or rather accursed, with an intellect *very* far superior to that of his race. Of course, he would be conscious of his superiority; nor could he (if otherwise constituted as man is) help manifesting his consciousness. Thus he would make himself enemies at all points. And since his opinions and speculations would widely differ from those of *all* mankind—that he would be considered a madman, is evident. How horribly painful such a condition! Hell could invent no greater torture than that of being charged with abnormal weakness on account of being abnormally strong.

In like manner, nothing could be clearer than that of a *very* generous spirit—*truly* feeling what all merely profess—must inevitably find itself misconceived in every direction—its motives misinterpreted. Just as extremeness of intelligence would be thought fatuity, so excess of chivalry could not fail of being looked upon as meanness in its last degree:—and so on with other virtues. The subject is a painful one indeed. That individuals *have* so soared above the plane of their race, is scarcely to be questioned: but, in looking back through history for traces of their existence, we should pass over all biographies of "the good and the great," while we search carefully the slight records of wretches who died in prison, in Bedlam, or upon the gallows.

THE WORLD OF OUR SAD HUMANITY . . .

There are moments when, even to the sober eyes of Reason, the world of our sad humanity must assume the aspect of Hell; but the Imagination of Man is no Carathis, to explore with impunity its every cavern. Alas! the grim legion of sepulchral terrors can*not* be regarded as altogether fanciful; but like the Demons in whose company Afrasiab made his voyage down the Oxus, they must sleep, or they will devour us—they must be suffered to slumber, or we perish.

A DENIZEN OF THE UNIVERSE

An infinity of error makes its way into our Philosophy, through Man's habit of considering himself a citizen of a world solely—of an individual planet—instead of at least occasionally contemplating his position as a cosmopolite proper—as a denizen of the universe.

Prose, Essays & Reviews

A DREAM

A few evenings since, I laid myself down for my night's repose. It has been a custom with me, for years past, to peruse a portion of the scriptures before I close my eyes in the slumbers of night. I did so in the present instance. By chance, I fell upon the spot where inspiration has recorded the dying agonies of the God of Nature. Thoughts of these, and the scenes which followed his giving up the ghost, pursued me as I slept.

There is certainly something mysterious and incomprehensible in the manner in which the wild vagaries of the imagination often arrange themselves; but the solution of this belongs to the physiologist rather than the reckless "dreamer."

It seemed that I was some Pharisee, returning from the scene of death. I had assisted in driving the sharpest nails through the palms of Him who hung on the cross, a spectacle of the bitterest woe that mortality ever felt. I could hear the groan that ran through his soul, as the rough iron grated on the bones when I drove it through. I retired a few steps from the place of execution, and turned around to look at my bitterest enemy. The Nazarene was not yet dead: the life lingered in the mantle of clay, as if it shuddered to walk alone through the valley of death. I thought I could see the cold damp settle on the brow of the dying, now standing in large drops on his. I could see each muscle quiver:—The eye, that began to lose its lustre in the hollow stare of the corpse. I could hear the low gurgle in his throat. —A moment,—and the chain of existence was broken, and a link dropped into eternity.

I turned away, and wandered listlessly on, till I came to the centre of Jerusalem. At a short distance rose the lofty turrets of the Temple; its golden roof reflected rays as bright as the source from which they emanated. A feeling of conscious pride stole over me, as I looked over the broad fields and lofty mountains which surrounded this pride of the eastern world. On my right rose Mount Olivet, covered with shrubbery and vineyards; beyond that, and bounding the skirts of mortal vision, appeared mountains piled on mountains; on the left were the lovely plains of Judea; and I thought it was a bright picture of human existence, as I saw the little brook of Cedron speeding its way through the meadows, to the distant lake. I could hear the gay song of the beauteous maiden, as she gleaned in the distant harvest-field; and, mingling with the echoes of the mountain, was heard the shrill whistle of the shepherd's pipe, as he called the wandering lamb to its fold. A perfect loveliness had thrown itself over animated nature.

But, "a change soon came o'er the spirit of my dream;" I felt a sudden coldness creeping over me. I instinctively turned toward the sun, and saw a hand slowly drawing a mantle cape over it. I looked for stars; but each one had ceased to twinkle; for the same hand had enveloped them in the badge of mourning. The silver light of the moon did not dawn on the sluggish waves of the Dead Sea, as they sang the hoarse requiem of the cities of the plain; but she hid her face as if shuddering to look on what was doing on the earth. I heard a muttered groan, as the spirit of darkness spread his pinions over an astonished world.

Unutterable despair now seized me. I could feel the flood of life slowly rolling back to its fountain, as the fearful thought stole over me, that the day of retribution had come. Suddenly, I stood before the temple. The veil, which had hid its secrets from unhallowed gaze, was now rent. I looked for a moment: the priest was standing by the altar, offering up the expiatory sacrifice. The fire, which was to kindle up the mangled limbs of the victim, gleamed for a moment, on the distant walls, and then 'twas lost in utter darkness. He turned around, to rekindle it from the living fire of the candlestick; but that, too, was gone.—'Twas still as the sepulchre.

I turned, and rushed into the street. The street was vacant. No sound broke the stillness, except the yell of the wild dog, who revelled on the half-burnt corpse in the Valley of Hinnom. I saw a light stream from a distant window, and made my way toward it. I looked in at the open door. A widow was preparing the last morsel she could glean, for the dying babe. She had kindled a little fire; and I saw with what utter hopelessness of heart she beheld the flame sink away, like her own dying hopes.

Darkness covered the universe. Nature mourned, for its parent had died. The earth had enrobed herself in the habiliments of sorrow, and the heavens were clothed in the sables of mourning. I now roamed in restlessness, and heeded not whither I went. At once there appeared a light in the east. A column of light shot athwart the gloom, like the light-shot gleams on the darkness of the mid-night of the pit, and illuminated the sober murkiness that surrounded me. There was an opening in the vast arch of heaven's broad expanse. With wondering eyes, I turned towards it.

Far into the wilderness of space, and at a distance that can only be meted by a "line running parallel with eternity," but still awfully plain and distinct, appeared the same person whom I had clothed with the mock purple of royalty. He was now garmented in the robe of the King of kings. He sat on his throne; but 'twas not one of whiteness. There was mourning in heaven; for, as each angel knelt before him, I saw that the wreath of immortal amaranth which was wont to circle his brow, was changed for one of cypress.

I turned to see whither I had wandered. I had come to the burial ground of the monarch of Israel. I gazed with trembling, as I saw the clods which covered the mouldering bones of some tyrant begin to move. I looked at where the last monarch had been laid, in all the splendour and pageantry of death, and the sculptured monument began to tremble. Soon it was overturned, and from it issued the tenant of the grave. 'Twas a hideous, unearthly form, such as Dante, in his wildest flights of terrified fancy, ne'er conjured up. I could not move, for terror had tied up volition. It approached me. I saw the grave-worm twining among the matted locks which in part covered the rotten skull. The bones creaked on each other as they moved on the hinges, for its flesh was gone. I listened to their horrid music, as this parody on poor mortality stalked along. He came up to me; and, as he passed, he breathed the cold damps of the lonely, narrow house directly in my face. The chasm in the heavens closed; and, with a convulsive shudder, I awoke.

[*1831*]

THE IMP OF THE PERVERSE

In the consideration of the faculties and impulses—of the *prima mobilia* of the human soul, the phrenologists have failed to make room for a propensity which, although obviously existing as a radical, primitive, irreducible sentiment, has been equally overlooked by all the moralists who have preceded them. In the pure arrogance of the reason, we have all overlooked it. We have suffered its existence to escape our senses, solely through want of belief—of faith;—whether it be faith in Revelation, or faith in the Kabbala. The idea of it has never occurred to us, simply because of its supererogation. We saw no *need* of the impulse—for the propensity. We could not perceive its necessity. We could not understand, that is to say, we could not have understood, had the notion of this *primum mobile* over obtruded itself;—we could not have understood in what manner it might be made to further the objects of humanity, either temporal or eternal. It cannot be denied that phrenology and, in great measure, all metaphysicianism have been concocted *a priori.* The intellectual or logical man, rather than the understanding or observant man, set himself to imagine designs—to dictate purposes to God. Having thus fathomed, to his satisfaction, the intentions of Jehovah, out of these intentions he built his innumerable systems of mind. In the matter of phrenology, for example, we first determined, naturally enough, that it was the design of the Deity that man should eat. We then assigned to man an organ of alimentiveness, and this organ is the scourge with which the Deity compels man, will-I nill-I, into eating. Secondly, having settled it to be God's will that man should continue his species, we discovered an organ of amativeness, forthwith. And so with combativeness, with ideality, with causality, with constructiveness,—so, in short, with every organ, whether representing a propensity, a moral sentiment, or a faculty of the pure intellect. And in these arrangements of the *principia* of human action, the Spurzheimites, whether right or wrong, in part, or upon the whole, have but followed, in principle, the footsteps of their predecessors; deducing and establishing every thing from the preconceived destiny of man, and upon the ground of the objects of his Creator.

It would have been wiser, it would have been safer to classify, (if classify we must,) upon the basis of what man usually or occasionally did, and was always occasionally doing, rather than upon the basis of what we took it for granted the Deity intended him to do. If we cannot comprehend God in his visible works, how then in his inconceivable thoughts, that call the works into being? If we cannot understand him in his objective creatures, how then in his substantive moods and phases of creation?

Induction, *a posteriori*, would have brought phrenology to admit, as an innate and primitive principle of human action, a paradoxical something, which we may call *perverseness*, for want of a more characteristic term. In the sense I intend, it is, in fact, a *mobile* without motive, a motive not *motivirt*. Through its promptings we act without comprehensible object; or, if this shall be understood as a contradiction in terms, we may so far modify the proposition as to say, that through its promptings we act, for the reason that we should *not*. In theory, no reason can be more unreasonable; but in fact, there is none more strong. With certain minds, under certain conditions, it becomes absolutely irresistible. I am not more certain that I breathe, than that the assurance of the wrong or error of any action is often the one unconquerable *force* which impels us, and alone impels us to its prosecution. Nor will this overwhelming tendency to do wrong for the wrong's sake, admit of analysis, or resolution into ulterior elements. It is a radical, a primitive impulse—elementary. It will be said, I am aware, that when we persist in acts because we feel we should *not* persist in them, our conduct is but a modification of that which ordinarily springs from the *combativeness* of phrenology. But a glance will show the fallacy of this idea. The phrenological combativeness has for its essence, the necessity of self-defence. It is our safeguard against injury. Its principle regards our well-being; and thus the desire to be well is excited simultaneously with its development. It follows, that the desire to be well must be excited simultaneously with any principle which shall be merely a modification of combativeness, but in the case of that something which I term *perverseness*, the desire to be well is not only not aroused, but a strongly antagonistical sentiment exists.

An appeal to one's own heart is, after all, the best reply to the sophistry just noticed. No one who trustingly consults and thoroughly questions his own soul, will be disposed to deny the entire radicalness of the propensity in question. It is not more incomprehensible than distinctive. There lives no man who at some period has not been tormented, for example, by an earnest desire to tantalize a listener by circumlocution. The speaker is aware that he displeases; he has every intention to please; he is usually curt, precise, and clear; the most laconic and luminous language is struggling for utterance upon his tongue; it is only with difficulty that he restrains himself from giving it flow; he dreads and deprecates the anger of him whom he addresses; yet the thought strikes him, that by certain involutions and parentheses, this anger may be engendered. That single thought is enough. The impulse increases to a wish, the wish to a desire, the desire to an uncontrollable longing, and the longing, (to the deep regret and mortification of the speaker, and in defiance of all consequences,) is indulged.

We have a task before us which must be speedily performed. We know that it will be ruinous to make delay. The most important crisis of our life calls, trumpet-tongued, for immediate energy and action. We glow, we are consumed with eagerness to commence the work, with the anticipation of whose glorious result our whole souls are on fire. It must, it shall be undertaken to-day, and yet we put it off until to-morrow; and why? There is no answer, except that we feel *perverse*, using the word with no comprehension of the principle. To-morrow arrives, and with it a more impatient anxiety to do our duty, but with this very increase of anxiety arrives, also, a nameless, a positively fearful because unfathomable, craving for delay. This craving gathers strength as the moments fly. The last hour for action is at hand. We tremble with the violence of the conflict within us,—of the definite with the indefinite—of the substance with the shadow. But, if the contest have proceeded thus far, it is the shadow which prevails,—we struggle in vain. The clock strikes, and is the knell of our welfare. At the same time, it is the chanticleer-note to the ghost that has so long overawed us. It flies—it disappears—we are free. The old energy returns. We will labor *now*. Alas, it is *too late!*

We stand upon the brink of a precipice. We peer into the abyss—we grow sick and dizzy. Our first impulse is to shrink from the danger. Unaccountably we remain. By slow degrees our sickness, and dizziness, and horror, become merged in a cloud of unnameable feeling. By gradations, still more imperceptible, this cloud assumes shape, as did the vapor from the bottle out of which arose the genius in the Arabian Nights. But out of this *our* cloud upon the precipice's edge, there grows into palpability, a shape, far more terrible than any genius, or any demon of a tale, and yet it is but a thought, although a fearful one, and one which chills the very marrow of our bones with the fierceness of the delight of its horror. It is merely the idea of what would be our sensations during the sweeping precipitancy of a fall from such a height. And this fall—this rushing annihilation—for the very reason that it involves that one most ghastly and loathsome of all the most ghastly and loathsome images of death and suffering which have ever presented themselves to our imagination—for this very cause do we now the most vividly desire it. And because our reason violently deters us from the brink, *therefore*, do we the more impetuously approach it. There is no passion in nature so demoniacally impatient, as that of him, who shuddering upon the edge of a precipice, thus meditates a plunge. To indulge for a moment, in any attempt at *thought*, is to be inevitably lost; for reflection but urges us to forbear, and *therefore* it is, I say, that we *cannot*. If there be no friendly arm to check us, or if we fail in a sudden effort to prostrate ourselves backward from the abyss, we plunge, and are destroyed.

Examine these and similar actions as we will, we shall find them resulting solely from the spirit of the *Perverse*. We perpetrate them merely because we feel that we should *not*. Beyond or behind this, there is no intelligible principle: and we might, indeed, deem this perverseness a direct instigation of the arch-fiend, were it not occasionally known to operate in furtherance of good.

I have said thus much, that in some measure I may answer your question—that I may explain to you why I am here—that I may assign to you something that shall have at least the faint aspect of a cause for my wearing these fetters, and for my tenanting this cell of the condemned. Had I not been thus prolix, you might either have misunderstood me altogether, or, with the rabble, have fancied me mad. As it is, you will easily perceive that I am one of the many uncounted victims of the Imp of the Perverse.

It is impossible that any deed could have been wrought with a more thorough deliberation. For weeks, for months, I pondered upon the means of the murder. I rejected a thousand schemes, because their accomplishment involved a *chance* of detection. At length, in reading some French memoirs, I found an account of a nearly fatal illness that occurred to Madame Pilau, through the agency of a candle accidentally poisoned. The idea struck my fancy at once. I knew my victim's habit of reading in bed. I knew, too, that his apartment was narrow and ill-ventilated. But I need not vex you with impertinent details. I need not describe the easy artifices by which I substituted, in his bed-room candlestand, a wax-light of my own making, for the one which I there found. The next morning he was discovered dead in his bed, and the coroner's verdict was,—"Death by the visitation of God."

Having inherited his estate, all went well with me for years. The idea of detection never once entered my brain. Of the remains of the fatal taper, I had myself carefully disposed. I had left no shadow of a clue by which it would be possible to convict, or even to suspect me of the crime. It is inconceivable how rich a sentiment of satisfaction arose in my bosom as I reflected upon my absolute security. For a very long period of time, I was accustomed to revel in this sentiment. It afforded me more real delight than all the mere worldly advantages accruing from my sin. But there arrived at length an epoch, from which the pleasurable feeling grew, by scarcely perceptible gradations, into a haunting and harassing thought. It harassed because it haunted. I could scarcely get rid of it for an instant. It is quite a common thing to be thus annoyed with the ringing in our ears, or rather in our memories, of the burthen of some ordinary song, or some unimpressive snatches from an opera. Nor will we be less tormented if the song in itself be good, or the opera air meritorious. In this manner, at last, I would perpetually catch myself pondering upon my security, and repeating, in a low, under-tone, the phrase, "I am safe."

One day, whilst sauntering along the streets, I arrested myself in the act of murmuring, half aloud, these customary syllables. In a fit of petulance, I re-modelled them thus:—"I am safe—I am safe—yes—if I be not fool enough to make open confession!"

No sooner had I spoken these words, than I felt an icy chill creep to my heart. I had had some experience in these fits of perversity, (whose nature I have been at some trouble to explain,) and I remembered well, that in no instance, I had successfully resisted their attacks. And now my own casual self-suggestion, that I might possibly be fool enough to confess the murder of which I had been guilty, confronted me, as if the very ghost of him whom I had murdered—and beckoned me on to death.

At first, I made an effort to shake off this nightmare of the soul. I walked vigorously—faster—still faster—at length I ran. I felt a maddening desire to shriek aloud. Every succeeding wave of thought overwhelmed me with new terror, for, alas! I well, too well understood that, to *think* in my situation, was to be lost. I still quickened my pace. I bounded like a madman through the crowded thoroughfares. At length, the populace took the alarm, and pursued me. I felt *then* the consummation of my fate. Could I have torn out my tongue, I would have done it—but a rough voice resounded in my ears—a rougher grasp seized me by the shoulder. I turned—I gasped for breath. For a moment, I experienced all the pangs of suffocation; I became blind, and deaf, and giddy; and then, some invisible fiend, I thought, struck me with his broad palm upon the back. The long-imprisoned secret burst forth from my soul.

They say that I spoke with a distinct enunciation, but with marked emphasis and passionate hurry, as if in dread of interruption before concluding the brief but pregnant sentences that consigned me to the hangman and to hell.

Having related all that was necessary for the fullest judicial conviction, I fell prostrate in a swoon.

But why shall I say more? To-day I wear these chains, and am *here*. To-morrow I shall be fetterless!—*but where?*

[*1845*]

Le Mystère de Marie Roget illustrated by Harry Clarke for Poe's TALES OF MYSTERY AND IMAGINATION, 1935

INSTINCT VS REASON—A BLACK CAT

The line which demarcates the instinct of the brute creation from the boasted reason of man, is, beyond doubt, of the most shadowy and unsatisfactory character—a boundary line far more difficult to settle than even the North-Eastern or the Oregon. The question whether the lower animals do or do not reason, will possibly never be decided—certainly never in our present condition of knowledge. While the self-love and arrogance of man will persist in denying the reflective power to beasts, because the granting it seems to derogate from his own vaunted supremacy, yet he perpetually finds himself involved in the paradox of decrying instinct as an inferior faculty, while he is forced to admit its infinite superiority, in a thousand cases, over the very reason which he claims exclusively as his own. Instinct, so far from being an inferior reason, is perhaps the most exacted intellect of all. It will appear to the true philosopher as the divine mind itself acting *immediately* upon its creatures.

The habits of the lion-ant, of many kinds of spiders, and of the beaver, have in them a wonderful analogy, or rather similarity, to the usual operations of the reason of man—but the instinct of some other creatures has no such analogy—and is referable only to the spirit of the Deity itself, acting *directly*, and through no corporal organ, upon the volition of the animal. Of this lofty species of instinct the coral-worm affords a remarkable instance. This little creature, the architect of continents, is not only capable of building ramparts against the sea, with a precision of purpose, and scientific adaptation and arrangement, from which the most skillful engineer might imbibe his best knowledge—but is gifted with what humanity does not possess—with the absolute spirit of prophecy. It will forsee, for months in advance, the pure accidents which are to happen in its dwelling, and aided by myriads of its brethren, all acting as if with one mind (and *indeed* acting with only one—with the mind of the Creator) will work diligently to counteract influences which exist alone in the future. There is also an immensely wonderful consideration connected with the cell of the bee. Let a mathematician be required to solve the problem of the shape best calculated in such a cell as the bee wants, for the two requisites of strength and space—and he will find himself involved in the very highest and most abstruse questions of analytical research. Let him be required to tell the number of sides which will give to the cell the greatest space, with the greatest solidity, and to define the exact angle at which, with the same object in view, the roof must incline—and to answer the query, he must be a Newton or a Laplace. Yet since bees were, they have been continually solving the problem. The leading distinction between instinct and reason seems to be, that, while the one is infinitely the more exact, the more certain, and the more far-seeing in its sphere of action—the sphere of action in the other is of the far wider extent. But we are preaching a homily, when we merely intended to tell a short story about a cat.

The writer of this article is the owner of one of the most remarkable black cats in the world—and this is saying much; for it will be remembered that black cats are all of them witches. The one in question has not a white hair about her, and is of a demure and sanctified demeanor. That portion of the kitchen which she most frequents is accessible only by a door, which closes with what is termed a thumb-latch; these latches are rude in construction, and some force and dexterity are always requisite to force them down. But puss is in the daily habit of opening the door, which she accomplishes in the following way. She first springs from the ground to the guard of the latch (which resembles the guard over a gun-trigger,) and through this she thrusts her left arm to hold on with. She now, with her right hand, presses the thumb-latch until it yields, and here several attempts are frequently requisite. Having forced it down, however, she seems to be aware that her task is but half accomplished, since, if the door is not pushed open before she lets go, the latch will again fall into its socket. She, therefore, screws her body round so as to bring her hind feet immediately beneath the latch, while she leaps with all her strength from the door—the impetus of the spring forcing it open, and her hind feet sustaining the latch until this impetus is fairly given.

We have witnessed this singular feat a hundred times at least, and never without being impressed with the truth of the remark with which we commenced this article—that the boundary between instinct and reason is of a very shadowy nature. The black cat, in doing what she did, must have made use of all the perceptive and reflective faculties which we are in the habit of supposing the prescriptive qualities of reason alone.

SHELLEY AND THE POETIC ABANDON

If ever mortal "wrecked his thoughts upon expression" it was *Shelley*. If ever poet sang—as a bird sings—earnestly—impulsively—with utter abandonment—to himself solely—and for the mere joy of his own song—that poet was the author of "The Sensitive Plant." Of Art—beyond that which is instinctive with Genius—he either had little or disdained all. He *really* disdained that Rule which is an emanation from Law, because his own soul was Law in itself. His rhapsodies are but the rough notes—the stenographic memoranda of poems—memoranda which, because they were not all-sufficient for his own intelligence, he cared not to be at the trouble of writing out in full for mankind. In all his works we find no conception thoroughly wrought. For this reason he is the most fatiguing of poets. Yet he wearies in saying too little rather than too much. What, in him, seems the diffuseness of one idea, is the conglomerate concision of many: and this species of concision it is, which renders him obscure. With such a man, to imitate was out of the question. It would have served no purpose; for he spoke to his own spirit alone, which would have comprehended no alien tongue. Thus he was profoundly original. His quaintness arose from intuitive perception of that truth to which Bacon alone has given distinct utterance:—"There is no exquisite Beauty which has not some strangeness in its proportions." But whether obscure, original, or quaint, Shelley had no *affectations*. He was at all times sincere.

From his *ruins*, there sprang into existence, affronting the heavens, a tottering and fantastic *pagoda*, in which the salient angels, tipped with mad jangling bells, were the idiosyncratic *faults* of the original—faults which cannot be considered such in view of his purposes, but which are monstrous when we regard his works as addressed to mankind. A "school" arose—if that absurd term must still be employed—a school—a system of *rules*—upon the basis of the Shelley who had none. Young men innumerable, dazzled by the glare and bewildered by the *bizarrerie* of the lightning that flickered through the clouds of "Alastor" had no trouble whatever in heaping up imitative vapors, but, for the lightning, were forced to be content with its *spectrum*, in which the *bizarrerie* appeared without the fire. Nor were mature minds unimpressed by the contemplation of a greater and more mature; and thus, gradually, into this school of all Lawlessness—or obscurity, quaintness and exaggeration—were interwoven the out-of-place didacticism of Wordsworth, and the more anomalous metaphysicianism of Coleridge. Matters were now fast verging to their worst; and at length, in *Tennyson* poetic inconsistency attained its extreme. But it was precisely this extreme (for the greatest truth and the greatest error are scarcely two points in a circle) which, following the law of all extremes, wrought in him (Tennyson) a natural and inevitable revulsion; leading him first to contemn, and secondly to investigate, his early manner, and finally to winnow, from its magnificent elements, the truest and purest of all poetical styles. But not even yet is the process complete; and for this reason in part, but chiefly on account of the mere fortuitousness of that mental and moral combination which shall unite in one person (if *ever* it shall) the Shelleyan *abandon* and the Tennysonian poetic sense, with the most profound Art (based both in Instinct and *Analysis*) and the sternest Will properly to blend and rigorously to control all—chiefly, I say, because such combinations of seeming antagonisms will only be a "happy chance"—the world has never yet seen the noblest poem which, possibly, *can* be composed.

THE FLAME OF LOVE
(*Byron and Miss Chaworth*)

"Les Anges," says Madame Dudevant [George Sand], a woman who intersperses many an admirable sentiment amid a chaos of the most shameless and altogether objectionable fiction—"*Les anges ne sont plus pures que le coeur d'un jeune homme qui aime en vérité.*" The angels are not more pure than the heart of a young man who loves with fervor.

The hyperbole is scarcely less than true. It would be truth itself, were it averred of the love of him who is at the same time young, and a poet. The boyish poet-love is indisputably that one of the human sentiments which most nearly realizes our dream of the chastened voluptuousness of heaven.

In every allusion made by the author of "Childe Harold" to his passion for Mary Chaworth, there runs a vein of almost spiritual tenderness and purity, strangely in contrast with the gross earthliness pervading and disfiguring his ordinary love poems. The Dream, in which the incidents of his parting with her when about to travel, are said to be delineated, or at least paralleled, has never been excelled (certainly never excelled by him) in the blended fervor, delicacy, truthfulness and ethereality which sublimate and adorn it. For this reason, it may well be doubted if he has written anything so universally popular.

That his attachment for this "Mary" (in whose very name there indeed seemed to exist for him an "enchantment") was earnest, and long-abiding, we have every reason to believe. There are a hundred evidences of this fact, scattered not only through his own poems and letters, but in the memoirs of his relatives, and contemporaries in general. But that it *was* thus earnest and enduring, does not controvert, in any degree, the opinion that it was a passion (if passion it can properly be termed) of the most thoroughly romantic, shadowy and imaginative character. It was born of the hour, and of the youthful necessity to love, while it was nurtured by the waters and the hills, the flowers and the stars. It had no peculiar regard to the person, or to the character, or to the reciprocating affection of Mary Chaworth. Any maiden, not immediately and positively repulsive, he would have loved, under the same circumstances of hourly and unrestricted communion, such as our engraving shadows forth. They met without restraint and without reserve. As mere children they sported together; in boyhood and girlhood they read from the same books, sang the same songs, or roamed, hand in hand, through the grounds of the conjoining estates. The result was not merely natural or merely probable, it was as inevitable as destiny itself.

In view of a passion thus engendered, Miss Chaworth, (who is represented as possessed of no little personal beauty and some accomplishments,) could not have failed to serve sufficiently well as the incarnation of the ideal that haunted the fancy of the poet. It is perhaps better, nevertheless, for the mere romance of the love-passages between the two, that their intercourse was broken up in early life and never uninterruptedly resumed in after years. Whatever of warmth, whatever of soul-passion, whatever of the truer nare and essentiality of romance was elicited during the youthful association is to be altogether attributed to the poet. If *she* felt at all, it was only while the magnetism of *his* actual presence compelled her to feel. If she responded at all, it was merely because the necromancy of *his* words of fire could not do otherwise than exhort a response. In absence, the bard bore easily with him all the fancies which were the basis of his flame—a flame which absence itself but served to keep in vigor—while the less ideal but at the same time the less really substantial affection of his ladye-love, perished utterly and forthwith, through simple lack of the element which had fanned it into being. He to her, in brief, was a not unhandsome, and not ignoble, but somewhat portionless, somewhat eccentric and rather lame young man. She to him was the Egeria of his dreams—the Venus Aphrodite that sprang, in full and supernal loveliness, from the bright foam upon the storm-tormented ocean of his thoughts.

Originally entitled "Byron and Miss Chaworth," this essay accompanied an engraving of Lord Byron and Mary Chaworth in the Columbian Magazine *for December 1844.*

THE CHARACTERS OF SHAKESPEARE

In all commenting on Shakespeare, there has been a radical error, never yet mentioned. It is the error of attempting to expound his characters—to account for their actions—to reconcile his inconsistencies—not as if they were the coinage of a human brain, but as if they had been actual existences upon earth. We talk of Hamlet the man, instead of Hamlet the *dramatis persona*—of Hamlet that God, in place of Hamlet that Shakespeare created. If Hamlet had really lived, and if the tragedy were an accurate record of his deeds, from the record (with some trouble) we might, it is true, reconcile his inconsistencies and settle to our satisfaction his true character. But the task becomes the purest absurdity when we deal only with a phantom. It is not (then) the inconsistencies of the acting man which we have as a subject of discussion (although we proceed as if it were, and thus *inevitably* err,) but the whims and the vacillations—the conflicting energies and indolences of the poet. It seems to us little less than a miracle, that this obvious point should have been overlooked.

While on this topic we may as well offer an ill-considered opinion of our own as to the *intention of the poet* in the delineation of the Dane. It must have been well known to Shakespeare, that a leading feature in certain more intense classes of intoxication, (from whatever cause,) is an almost irresistible impulse to counterfeit a farther degree of excitement than actually exists. Analogy would lead any thoughtful person to suspect the same impulse in madness—where beyond doubt it is manifest. This, Shakespeare *felt*—not thought. He felt it through his marvelous power of *identification* with humanity at large—the ultimate source of his magical influence upon mankind. He wrote of Hamlet as if Hamlet he were; and having, in the first instance, imagined his hero excited to partial insanity by the disclosures of the ghost—he (the poet) *felt* that it was natural he should be impelled to exaggerate the insanity.

LE CORBEAU

(THE RAVEN)

Poème d'Edgar POE

Traduit par Stéphane MALLARMÉ

Illustré de cinq Dessins de MANET

TEXTE ANGLAIS ET FRANÇAIS

Illustrations sur Hollande ou sur Chine

AU CHOIX

Couverture et Ex-Libris en parchemin. — Tirage limité.

PRIX : 25 FRANCS.

Avec Épreuves doubles sur Hollande et Chine : 35 francs.

Cartonnage illustré, en sus : 5 francs.

The cover of the first French edition of *The Raven*, translated by Stéphane Mallarmé and illustrated by Edouard Manet.

THE FRENCH VIEW

THE FRENCH VIEW

Poor Edgar Allan Poe died translated,
In unpressed pants, ended in light,
Surrounded by ecstatic gold bugs,
His begira blessed by Baudelaire's orgy.
—Bob Kaufman

From Charles Baudelaire to the Surrealists, Poe was a catalyst.

Adopted first by Baudelaire and made the *cause célèbre* for his own wars against French literature and the bourgeoisie, Poe was for him an alter-ego, a long-lost brother, a partner in crime, and a writer in whom he could confide his sacred fury. Of the twelve volumes of Baudelaire's complete works, five are devoted to his brilliant translations of Poe.

Baudelaire was in his late twenties when he encountered Poe's work, and it is amusing to read his imaginary projection of who this American might be:

> "Two years before the catastrophe which so horribly destroyed his life, so full and so ardent, I had already undertaken to introduce Edgar Poe to the literary public of my own country. But at that time his ever-stormy life was unknown to me; I did not know that those dazzling growths sprung from a volcanic soil, and today when I compare the false idea I had conjured of his life with the reality,—the Edgar Poe of my imagination,—rich, happy, a young gentleman of genius who sometimes turned his hand to literature in the midst of countless activities of an elegant life,—when I compare that with the true Edgar . . . the ironic antithesis fills me with inescapable compassion. Several years have passed and I have been constantly obsessed by his ghost."

The role of wealthy aristocrat is not so far removed from either Poe or Baudelaire, both of whom stood to inherit considerable wealth but were cut off as a result of youthful squanderings. There is, in physical descriptions given by their contemporaries, an uncanny resemblance between Poe and Baudelaire—impeccable manners, gentility, suave grooming and dress (contrary to the popular opinion of the disheveled Bohemian), a cool detachment, but with a fixity of gaze that could melt ice and foe alike. And in the midst of poverty, both maintained the one requisite element of the dandy: elegance. Poe's anti-democratic views persuaded Baudelaire to abandon his socialism, and if these two men shared a single political preference it was monarchy. But each was a country unto himself, a majority of one, an aristocrat of the mind. There is arrogance here: the arrogance of loneliness.

In these essays, Baudelaire initiates many of the outlandish theories on which his own scandalous reputation was based. His analyses of Poe's works today remain fundamental and novel, particularly in their appreciation of Poe's *humor*, perhaps his most elusive trait.

Two decades later, Stéphane Mallarmé began translating Poe's poems into French, recreating in his own style the sonorities and rhythms of the originals. The Symbolist Mallarmé was attracted to the purity of the poems—the excessive refinement and hermetic air of, for example, "The Sleeper," "Dreamland," and "Sonnet to Silence," full of opium and incense, and to their crystalline quality:

> "So few lines of poetry at such long intervals—but in which the poet affirmed his entire peotic vision—should we reduce them further? Yes, in order to give the new reader attracted by the titles of these poems nothing but marvels. Thus, almost every one of the twenty poems is a unique masterpiece of its kind and produces in one of its facets glittering with strange fires, the thing that was always either flashing or translucent for Poe, pure as the diamond—poetry."

The purification of poetic language, removed from all political, moral, or educational elements, and Poe's dictum that a poem should have no object in view but *itself*, set the tone for the entire Symbolist movement.

From Mallarmé on, interpretations of Poe diverge radically. The Symbolists (Mallarmé, Kahn, Samain, de Gourmont, Moréas, Vielé-Griffin, Ghil, Valéry) adopt the Poe of ordered, pragmatic, rational thought—the master of formal investigation and the fine art of reasoning. On the other hand, the decadents (Huysmans, Villiers de l'Isle-Adam, Barbey d'Aurevilly, Gabriele d'Annunzio) and the pre-Surrealists (Rimbaud, Lautréamont, Jarry and Apollinaire) embrace the adventuresome Poe, the high priest of horror, mystery, imagination, dreams, drugs, and the disorders of the sensate mind.

One particular quality in Poe's writing took on cardinal importance: what the Surrealist André Breton called *convulsive beauty*,—violent, shattering, involuntary, and inclusive of the erotic. Just as the narrator of Poe's "The Oblong Box" ends his tale with the "hysterical laugh which will ring forever in my ears," there is a similarly nagging demon haunting the French writers, wreaking havoc with the senses, shifting the ground underfoot. Whether this demon takes the form of Huysmans' morbid obsessions or Paul Valéry's preoccupation with the quintessential algebraic sonnet, the grand architectural poem to end all poems, the aim is not dissimilar. It is a quest for that ideal Beauty which is *freedom*.

By no one is the quest for human emancipation more passionately articulated, or militantly insisted upon, than by André Breton. In the 1924 *Manifesto*, he hailed Poe as "surrealist in adventure," and later as "one of those explorers whom an insatiable desire carries to the verge of discovery—those for whom nothing matters except the continual surpassing of the goal already attained."

In truth, France's greatest poetic geniuses took Poe seriously, while he was generally misunderstood and derided in literary America. To French poets, Poe was more than just a model; he was a mirror from afar in which they saw themselves. For Baudelaire, Poe wandered lifelong drunken and deranged throughout a vast prison that was the United States, while Mallarmé thought of Poe as living a quiet life, like himself, "an existence simple and monotonous."

Here then, is the man and his shadow, cast across two continents and two centuries.

R.F.

Charles Baudelaire by French photographer, Nadar

From EDGAR POE: HIS LIFE AND WORKS
By Charles BAUDELAIRE

". . . some unhappy master, whom unmerciful Disaster
Followed fast and followed faster till his songs one burden bore—
Till the dirges of his Hope that melancholy burden bore
Of 'Never—nevermore!' "

Edgar Poe—The Raven

"Sur son trône d'airain le Destin, qui s'en raille,
Imbibe leur éponge avec du fiel amer,
Et la nécessité les tord dans sa tenaille."

[*"On its bronze throne, Destiny, who mocks them,*
Steeps their sponge in bitter gall,
And necessity twists them in its grip."]

Théophile Gautier—Ténèbres

I.

Recently in the courts, there appeared before the magistrates an unfortunate fellow, upon whose forehead was inscribed a strange and singular tattoo: *Born to Lose!* Thus above his eyes he bore the epigraphy of his life like the title of a book, and subsequent interrogation proved this bizarre inscription to be cruelly true. In the history of literature there are analogous destinies of actual damnation—men who bear the words "bad luck" etched in mysterious characters in the sinuous folds of their foreheads. The blind angel of Expiation has taken hold of them, brutally punishing them for the edification of others. In vain their loves show talents, virtues, graces; but society has a special anathema for them, even accusing them of the infirmities its own persecution has produced. What did Hoffman not do to disarm Destiny? What did Balzac not undertake to conjure Fortune? Does there not exist a diabolical Providence that plots misfortune from the cradle forward—that deliberately thrusts these spiritual and angelic beings into hostile surroundings, like martyrs into the arena? Can there be, then, sacred souls, doomed to the sacrificial altar, condemned to march to death and glory through the shambles of their own lives? Will the Nightmare of Darkness eternally besiege these chosen souls? In vain they battle, in vain try to conform to the world, to its collusions, and its schemes; even if they are perfect in discretion, batten-up every entry, bar the windows against the missiles of chance, the Demon will enter through a key-hole; some perfection shall be the flaw in their armor; some superior quality will be the germ of their damnation.

> "L'aigle, pour le briser, du haut du firmament,
> Sur leur front découvert lâchera la tortue,
> Cars ils doivent périr inévitablement."
>
> [*"To smash it, the eagle will drop a tortoise*
> *from on high, on their uncovered heads*
> *for they must inevitably perish."*[1]

Their destiny is inscribed in their very nature; it sparkles with a sinister gleam in their looks and in their gestures, running through their veins with every drop of blood.

A celebrated author of our day[2] has written a book to demonstrate that the poet is at a loss to find a just place either in a democratic or aristocratic society, in a republic or monarchy, absolute or otherwise. Who has responded to him satisfactorily? Today I add a new legend to support his thesis, I add a new saint to the martyrology; I write the story of an illustrious outcast, too rich with poetry and passion, who came, after so many others, to serve in this base world the harsh apprentice of genius among inferior souls.

What a lamentable tragedy the life of Edgar Poe! His death, a horrible end magnified by the guttered circumstances surrounding it! All the documents I have read strengthen my conviction that, for Poe, the United States was nothing more than a vast prison through which he wandered with the feverish unrest of one who was born to breathe the air of a purer world—a great and barbarous gas-lit nightmare—and that his inner spiritual life, as a poet or even as a drunkard, was but one perpetual effort to flee the influence of this hostile milieu. A pitiless dictator is public opinion in a democratic society; do not implore from it charity, nor indulgence, nor any flexibility in the application of its laws to the multifarious complexities of moral life. One might as well say that from the impious love of liberty a new tyranny is born, the tyranny of beasts, a zoöcracy, which, in its ferocious insensitivity resembles the idol of the Juggernaut. One biographer tells us gravely, and with the best of intentions, that Poe, had he been willing to regulate his genius and apply his creative faculties in a manner appropriate to the American soil, might have become *un auteur à argent*—a money-making author; another—this one a simple-minded cynic—held that as splendid as Poe's genius was, it would have been better for him had he possessed talent only, as talent pays with easier terms than genius. Another, an editor of magazines and newspapers, a friend of the poet, avowed that it was difficult to employ him; and he was obliged to pay him less than the others, because he wrote in a style over and above the vulgar head. "How this reeks of the market-place," as Joseph de Maistre[3] would say.

Some have even stooped lower, and, coupling the dullest incomprehension of his genius with the ferocity of bourgeois hypocrisy, have outdone their own insults, and, after his sudden passing, cruelly lectured his corpse; particularly Mr. Rufus Griswold, who, to quote George Graham's vengeful remark, "committed an immortal infamy." Poe, having perhaps a fatal presentiment of a sudden end, had designated Mr. Griswold and Mr. Willis to set his works in order, write his biography, and perpetuate his memory. The first—a pedagogic vampire—slandered his friend at length in an enormous, crass, and hateful article, prefixed to the posthumous edition of Poe's works. Does there not exist in America an ordinance to keep dogs out of the cemeteries? Mr. Willis has proved, on the contrary, that kindness and respect go hand in hand with true intelligence, and that charity toward our fellow men, which is ever a moral duty, is also one of the dictates of good taste.

Talk to an American about Poe and he will freely admit his genius, perhaps he will even display pride; but, in a sardonic and superior tone (being a practical man), he will speak of the depraved life of the poet, of the alcohol on his breath that could have been lit with a candle, of the habitual vagabond; he will tell of his erratic and heteroclite existence, a planet out of orbit, ceaselessly rushing from Baltimore to New York, New York to Philadelphia, Boston to Baltimore, Baltimore to Richmond. And then, if moved by these preludes of a despairing tale, you suggest the notion that he was perhaps not the only one guilty, and it must be difficult to think or write in a country that has millions of sovereigns, no national capital to speak of, and no aristocracy,—then you will see light and anger flash in his eyes, wounded patriotism frothing at his lips, and you will hear America, through his mouth, slinging insults at Europe, its venerated mother, and at the philosophy of ancient days.

I repeat my firm conviction that Edgar Poe and his country were not on the same level. The United States is a gigantic infant, naturally jealous of the older continent. Proud of its material development, abnormal and nearly monstrous, this newcomer in history has a naive faith in the almightiness of industry; it is convinced, like some wretches among us, that it will succeed in consuming the Devil himself. Time and money are national treasures! Material pursuit, exaggerated to proportions of a national mania, leaves little room in the mind for unworldly pursuits. Poe, who came from a good background, and moreover professed that the great misfortune of his country lay in the lack of an aristocracy (since in such a people the cult of the Beautiful could not fail to be corrupted, diminished, and die)—who accused his fellow citizens, in their exorbitant and gaudy luxury, with all the symptoms of bad taste characteristic of the lowborn; who considered Progress, that great modern invention, to be an ecstasy for dupes, and who called "home improvements" eyesores and rectangular abominations: Poe was of a singular and solitary mind there. He believed in the immutable, the eternal, the "selfsame," and (like Machiavelli) he enjoyed—cruel privilege in a society infatuated with itself—healthy good sense which marches before the wise man like a column of fire across the desert of history. What would he have thought, what would he have written, if he had heard of the theologian of sentiment[4] who, out of love for the human race, suppressed Hell itself; or the philosopher of numbers who proposed an insurance system, a contribution of a penny per person, to get rid of war; and the abolition of the death penalty and of orthography, those two correlative follies!—and so many authors who write, with their ears to the wind, derivative fantasies as flatulent as the ambitions that bring them into being? If you add to this an impeccable vision of truth, an actual handicap under certain circumstances, an exquisite delicacy of taste revolted by all except exact proportions, an insatiable love of the Beautiful, which had assumed the force of a morbid passion, you will not be astonished that for such a man as this life became a hell, and a dead end; no, you will be amazed that he *endured* for such a long time.

II.

(Baudelaire's inaccurate reconstruction of Poe's biography which begins this section is omitted here.)

Poe's death is almost a suicide—a suicide a long time in preparation. At any rate, it caused that kind of scandal. There was a grand outcry, and *virtue* carried on its obsessive *cant*, freely and voluptuously. The more indulgent funeral orations could only give way to the inevitable bourgeois moralizing, which was quick to seize such a perfect opportunity. Mr. Griswold slandered him; Mr. Willis, sincerely grieved, behaved more than just appropriately. Alas! The man who had surmounted the most arduous esthetic heights, and plunged into the abysses least explored by the human intellect, who throughout a life that resembled a tempest with no calm, had invented new forms, unknown avenues to astonish the imagination, to captivate all minds desiring beauty, died fleetingly in a hospital bed—ah fate! Such consummate grandeur, such misfortune, to stir up an eddy of bourgeois pronouncements, all this become the theme and fodder for virtuous journalists!

Ut declamatio fias!

Such spectacles are not new; it is rare for newly entombed illustrious ones *not* to be subject of scandal. Society, moreover, shrinks from these mad unfortunates, and, whether it be that they trouble its holidays, or it suffers naive remorse, in either case, society is uncontestably in the right. Who will fail to recall the declaimers in Paris at the time of Balzac's death, despite a respectable end? And still more recently—just one year ago today, when an admirably honest writer, highly intelligent, *who was always lucid*, discreetly, disturbing no one, so much so that his discretion resembled contempt, freed his soul in the darkest alley he could find.[5] What degrading sermons!—what refined assassinations! One eminent journalist (who will never learn philanthropy from Jesus), found the occasion jovial enough to contrive a gross pun. In the many enumerations of the rights of man which nineteenth century sagacity proliferates so complacently, two most important ones have been overlooked; the right to contradict one's self, and the right to take one's life. Ah, but society regards as insolent those who so take their leave; she would gladly chastise their mortal remains, like that unlucky soldier become a vampire, frothing in fury at the sight of a corpse. And yet we might say that, under the pressure of certain circumstances, given serious examination of certain incompatibilities, with firm belief in certain dogmas and metempsychoses, we might say without bombast or fanciful words, that suicide is sometimes the most reasonable act in life. And thus is formed a fraternity of already innumerable phantoms, which haunts us intimately, each member of which comes to praise his present repose, and convert us with his beliefs.

We must admit that the gloomy end of the author of *Eureka* did provoke some consoling exceptions, without which we would most deeply despair, and find things bearable no longer. Mr. Willis, as I have said, spoke honestly and with emotion, of the good relations he had always had with Poe. John Neal and George Graham recalled Griswold to shame. Mr. Longfellow, who is all the more commendable as Poe had harshly affronted him, praised in a manner worthy of a poet Poe's power as poet and prose writer. And an anonymous writer said that American literature had lost its finest mind.

But the broken heart, the heart torn apart, the heart pierced by the seven swords was that of Mrs. Clemm. Edgar was at once her son and daughter. Cruel destiny, said Willis, from whom I borrow these details almost word for word, It was a cruel destiny that she watched over and sheltered. For Edgar Poe was a difficult man; he wrote with fastidious standards and in a style too far above the average intellect to be fairly paid; and he was always deluged with financial embarrassment, while he and his ailing wife lacked the very necessities of life. At Willis' office one day there arrived a woman—old, sweet, solemn. It was Mrs Clemm. She was *seeking work* for her dear Edgar. The biographer says that he was singularly impressed, not only by her perfect commendation, her clear appreciation for her son-in-law's gifts, but also by her whole appearance, the sound of her voice, sweet and sad, her manners old-fashioned, but refined and elegant. And for several years, he adds, he saw this indefatigable servant of genius, in want and poorly dressed, going from editor to editor for the purpose of selling a poem, or an article, saying *he* was sick, the only explanation, the sole reason, the invariable excuse she offered when her son labored under the sterile periods known intimately by turbulent writers,—never permitting to fall from her lips one syllable that could be interpreted as a doubt, a slackening of confidence in the genius and will of her beloved son. When her daughter died, she attached herself to him and watched over the disastrous battle with a reinforced maternal devotion, she lived with him and cared for him, sheltering him and defending him against life and against himself. Surely—Willis concludes with high and impartial reasoning—if ever the devotion of a woman, born of a first love, hallows and consecrates its object, what does not a devotion like this—pure, unselfish, and holy as a guardian angel—say for him who inspired it? Poe's detractors are at a loss to notice that there are some charms so powerful that they can only be truths.

Of the poor woman's anguish at the news we can only guess. She wrote a letter to Willis from which I quote these lines:

"I have this morning heard of the death of my beloved Eddie . . . I need not ask you to announce his death, and to speak well of him. I know you will. But say what an affectionate son he was to me his poor desolate mother . . ."

It appears to me that this woman is great, and has the grace of the Ancients. Struck by an irreparable loss, she thinks only of him who was everything to her. And it is not enough for her to have it said that he was a genius, it must be known also that he was a man of duty and affection. It is evident that this mother, a torch and hearth illuminated by a ray from Heaven, has been given as an example to the human race, as witness to devotion, to heroism, and all that which exceeds moral obligation. Was it not just to inscribe above the works of the poet the name of that woman who was the moral sun of his life?[6] His glory will enhance the name of the woman whose tenderness dressed his wounds, whose image will linger eternally above the martyrology of literature.

III.

Poe's life, his morals, his manners, his very being, all the elements that constituted his entire person, appear to us at once something both dark and brilliant. He was a singular and fascinating person, who, like his work, was marked with an indefinable stamp of melancholy. He was remarkably gifted in every way. As a boy, he displayed rare aptitude in all physical exercises, and although he was slight, with hands and feet like a woman's, his whole being had delicacy but was tough and capable of extraordinary feats of strength. As a boy, he won a wager for swimming a distance ordinarily considered impossible. One might say that Nature provides her chosen ones with an energetic stamina, just as she endows with an abundant vitality those trees which most symbolize hardship and grief. Such men, who sometimes appear slight, are built as athletes, fit for orgies as well as hard labor, quick to excesses and capable of startling sobriety.

Some things about Edgar Poe elicit unanimous accord; for example, his lofty natural distinction, his eloquence and physical beauty, about which it has been said he was more than a little vain. His manners, a unique blend of the aloof with an exquisite sweetness, were self-assured. His features, his bearing, his gestures, his countenance, all designated him, especially on his good days, as a favored creature. His entire being breathed a penetrating air of solemnity. He was truly marked by nature, like those passersby seen once in a glance who haunt the memory. Even the pedantic and spiteful Griswold concedes, that when he paid a visit to Poe, and found him pale and still ill over the death and illness of his wife, he was exceedingly struck, not only by the perfection of his manners, but moreover by his aristocratic air, the fragrant atmosphere of the apartment, although it was modestly furnished. Griswold is ignorant of the fact that the poet, more than other men, has that marvellous gift attributed to the women of Paris and Spain, the ability to dress well on nothing, and that Poe, lover of beauty in all things, would have the art of transforming a cottage into a palace of a special kind. Did he not write, with wit and originality and curious interest, of plans for furniture, country mansions, and landscape architecture?

(Omitted here is Baudelaire's quote from a lengthy letter by Mrs. Frances Osgood, verifying his own claims for Poe's diligence, graciousness, and devotion to his wife and their home.)

In Poe's stories, love does not speak its name. At least *Ligeia* or *Eleanora* are not, strictly speaking, love stories, as the principal idea on which the work pivots is something quite different. Perhaps he thought that prose was not a language elevated enough for that strange and nearly untranslatable sentiment; for his poems, in contrast, are richly saturated by it. There the divine passion shows itself magnificent, celestial, and ever shrouded in irredeemable melancholy. In his essays, he sometimes speaks of love, and even as he speaks its name, his pen trembles. In the *Domain of Arnheim* he declares the four conditions requisite to a happy life are: life in the open air, *the love of a woman*, detachment from all ambition, and the creation of a new beauty. What corroborates Mrs. Osgood's idea regarding Poe's chivalrous respect for women, in spite of his prodigious talent for horror and the grotesque, is that in the whole of his work there is not a single passage that exploits lust, or even sensual indulgence. His portraits of women are, so to speak, haloed; they radiate from a supernatural mist, painted with the hand of an adoring lover. As for the *petits épisodes romanesques*, why should it be astonishing that one so excitable, for whom the thirst for beauty was perhaps his principal trait, should sometimes, with passionate ardor, have cultivated gallantry, that volcanic and musk-like flower, for which the brain of the poet is a natural soil?

His strange and singular beauty is discussed in several biographies. I believe that it is possible to construct an approximate idea of his mind by conjuring vague, but nevertheless characteristic notions, contained in the word *romantic*, a word that is generally used to define a kind of beauty in which the facial expression is of special importance. Poe had a broad, dominating forehead, certain protuberances of which registered those abundant properties attributed to them—construction, comparison, causality—and where the sense of ideality, the esthetic sense *par excellence*, is enthroned in serene pride. Nevertheless, in spite of these gifts, or perhaps because of them, his head, seen in profile, did not have an entirely agreeable look. As with all things excessive in one sense, want can result from abundance, and poverty from generosity. His magnificent eyes were dark and luminous, indeterminate and somber in color, approaching violet, the nose was noble and firm, the mouth fine and sad, even when slightly smiling; his skin was a light brown, the face generally pale, his expression dreamy and subtly obscured by a habitual melancholy.

His conversation was most remarkable and fertile. He was not what one might call a "glib talker"—a horrible thing—indeed his speech, like his pen, had a horror of conventionalities; but his vast knowledge, his command of language, his serious studies, the impressions gathered from his travels in several countries made his talk enlightening. His eloquence, essentially poetic, highly methodical, and yet exceeding all accepted method, his arsenal of images drawn from a world seldom frequented by pedestrian minds, a prodigious art in drawing secret and novel deductions from an evident and absolutely acceptable proposition, in revealing astonishing new perspectives, and, in a phrase, the art of enchanting, unraveling thoughts, creating dreams, wrenching souls from the mire of routine—such was the dizzying facility of his thought so many people recalled. But it happened on occasion—or was said to—that the poet, compelled by destructive caprice, brusquely brought his friends to earth with a painful cynicism, brutally demolishing the impression of his spirituality. It is moreover worthy of note that he was not particular in his choice of listeners, and I believe that the reader will have no difficulty uncovering other intelligent, original authors in history for whom all kinds of company were acceptable.[7] Certain minds, alone in the crowd, retreat into inner monologue, not caring about the "refinement" of their public. It is, in short, a fraternity based on scorn.

As for his drunkenness,—celebrated and reproached with a self-righteousness that would give us the impression that all other writers in the United States, except Poe, are angels of sobriety. This needs to be addressed. Several accounts are plausible, and they are not mutually exclusive. Above all, I am obliged to remark that Willis and Mrs. Osgood have affirmed that the tiniest quantity of wine or liquor was enough to perturb the equilibrium of his constitution. It is, moreover, easy to assume that a man so truly alone, so profoundly despondent, and who must have envisioned the social system as a paradox and imposture, a man, who, badgered by a merciless fate, often referred to society as a throng of scoundrels (it is Griswold who reports this, scandalized as only a man can be who might have had the same thoughts but would never admit them),—it is natural, I contend, to suppose that this poet who as an infant was expelled into the hazards of an unrestrained life, his mind bound by long and hard drudgery, might sometimes seek the voluptuous oblivion found in a bottle. Literary rancors, deliria of infinity, problems at home, the insults of poverty . . . Poe fled all of these into that drunken night, as if rehearsing for the grave. But however credible this explanation, I do not think it sufficiently encompassing, and I distrust its deplorable simplicity.

I am told that he did not drink as a gourmand but as a barbarian, with a briskness and economy altogether American, as if to commit an act of murder, as if *something* in him had to be killed, *a worm that would not die*. Furthermore, it is reported that one day, when he was on the point of marrying a second time (the banns of marriage had been published, and, while being congratulated on this union which offered the highest conditions of good fortune and well being, he said: "It is possible that you have seen the banns of marriage, but note this well: I shall not marry!") He then went about appallingly drunk, scandalizing the neighborhood of his designated wife, providing thus recourse to his vice in order to rid himself of an act of disloyalty toward the dead woman whose image was alive in him always, and whom he had so wonderfully sung in his *Annabel Lee*. I consider then, in a great number of cases, the infinitely precious fact of premeditation is a certainty.

In a long article in the *Southern Literary Messenger*, a magazine whose success he initiated, I have read how the purity, the perfection of his style, the firmness and severity of his thought, his eagerness for work, were never changed by this terrible habit, how the creation of most of his outstanding pieces preceded or followed one of his crises; that after the publication of *Eureka*, he indulged deplorably in his inclination to drink, and in New York, on the very morning *The Raven* appeared, while the name of the poet was on the lips of all, he walked down Broadway, staggering outrageously. Take note of the words: *preceding* or *following*, intimating that his drunkenness could have been excitation as well as repose.

Now, it is incontestable that—(like those striking and fugitive impressions, most striking in their repetition when they are most fugitive, sometimes following some exterior sign, a kind of warning like the tolling of a bell, a musical note, a forgotten perfume, and which themselves follow events similar to others already known, occupying the same place in a previous chain of thoughts, just as strange repetitive dreams arise in our sleep)—there exists in drunkenness not solely the enchantment of dreams, but a rational sequence that, to recur again, would necessitate the milieu which inspired it.[8] If by now the reader has not been repulsed, he may have already divined my conclusion: I believe that very often, though certainly not always, Poe's inebriation was a mnemonic means, a method of work, a method drastic and deadly, yet appropriate to his passionate nature. The poet had learned to drink, just as a careful writer takes pains to keep notes. He could not resist the desire to recover marvellous or terrifying visions, subtle concepts encountered in a previous storm; they were old friends who lured him imperiously, and, to renew his contact with them, he took the most dangerous, but most direct road. The part of him which gives us joy today is that which slew him.

IV.

About the works of this singular genius I have very little to say; the public will soon show what it thinks. It would be difficult for me, but not impossible, to unravel his method, to explain his process, particularly in the part of his work where the main effect rests on well-drawn analysis. I could introduce the reader to the mysteries of his art, giving special attention to that part of American genius which made him rejoice over a difficulty conquered, an enigma explained, a successful tour-de-force—which encouraged him to gamble with a childlike and almost perverse pleasure in a world of probabilities and conjectures—and to invent *hoaxes* which his subtle art gives the reality of life itself. No one can deny that Poe is a marvellous *jongleur*, and yet I know the author esteemed another aspect of his work. I have some important remarks to make, and I will be brief.

It was not for these earthly miracles, however they brought him renown, that he won the admiration of thinkers, but for his love of the beautiful; his poetry, profound and melancholy, yet made crystal clear like a translucent gem—pure and strange—closely woven as the chain mail on armor, pleasing and thorough, the slightest turn of which served to impel the reader subtly toward a desired end; and, above all, by that very special genius, by that unique temperament which permitted him to paint and delineate, in an impeccable, chilling, and terrible manner, *the exception to the moral order.* Diderot, to choose one example in a hundred, is a red-blooded author; Poe was a writer of nerves, and of much more—and the best writer I know.

Poe's opening passages are always attractive, without violence, like a whirlpool. His solemnity surprises and keeps the mind on guard. We sense at once his gravity. And slowly, little by little, there unfolds a tale where all intrigue rests in an imperceptible deviation of intellect, an audacious hypothesis, and an imprudent dose by Nature of an amalgam of faculties. The reader, in a kind of vertigo, is constrained to follow the author through his successive deductions.

No man, I repeat, has told with greater magic the *exceptions* of human life and nature; the fevered curiosities of convalescence; the dying seasons charged with enervating splendors; the tropic zones; humid, hot, and misty days, where the south wind soothes and distends the nerves like the strings of an instrument, filling one's eyes with tears that do not come from the heart,—the hallucination welling first with doubt, but then convincing and rational as a book;—the absurd taking over the intellect and governing it with a frightful logic;—hysteria usurping the will; contradiction lying between nerves and intellect; and man deranged to the point of expressing grief with a grin. He analyzes what is most fugitive, weighs the imponderable, and describes, in a precise and scientific manner, effecting terror, all the imaginings that waft about the nerve-ridden man, leading him to destruction.

The ardor with which he hurls himself into the grotesque for the love of the grotesque and into the horrible for the love of the horrible, verifies the sincerity of his work, and aligns the man with the poet. I have already remarked that in many men this ardor was often the result of a vast unused life-force, sometimes the result of unremitting chastity, and also of a profoundly repressed sensibility. The supernatural delight that a man might feel looking at the flow of his own blood; sudden, violent, and impulsive movements; great cries uttered to dead air without being willed; all are phenomena of the same order.

In the rarefied air of this literature, the mind may feel the vague anguish, the fear that quickens into tears, the malaise of the heart that dwells in vast and lonely space. But our wonder is all the stronger; and, then, his art is so great! The backgrounds and props are all appropriate to the characters' feelings. The solitude of nature, or the turmoil of cities, all are described there, feverishly and fantastically. Like our own Eugene Delacroix, who has elevated his art to the height of great poetry, Edgar Poe loves to move his troubled figures against violet and green backdrops to reveal the phosphorescence of decay, and the odor of the storm. Inanimate nature takes part in the nature of living beings, and, like them, shudders a supernal and convulsive shudder. Space is fathomed by opium, for opium lends a sense of magic to all hues, and causes every noise to vibrate with the most sonorous magnificence. Now and then glorious vistas, imbued with light and color, unfold suddenly in his landscape and on the distant horizon we can see Oriental cities and palaces, ephemeral and distant, bathed in sunlight like a shower of gold.

Poe's characters, or rather *the* Poe character, a man of acute faculties, a man of cool nerves, a man whose ardent but patient will hurls defiance at obstacles, whose gaze is steadfast and unyielding like a rapier pointed at objects that intensify under his gaze—this is Poe himself. And his women, all luminous and ill, dying of strange diseases, speaking in voices like music—they are also he, or at least, by their strange aspirations, by their knowledge, by their incurable melancholy, they flow strongly out of their creator's nature. Regarding his ideal woman, his Titanide, she is revealed in different portraits scattered through his poems, so few in number—portraits, or rather modes of feeling beauty, which the temperament of the author fuses and blends in a vague yet real unity, where, more delicately than anywhere else, the insatiable love of Beauty lives, which is his true claim; it is the totality of his claim to the affection and respect of poets.

We have assembled under the title *Histoires Extraordinaires*, diverse tales chosen from the whole of Poe's work. His works are comprised of a considerable number of short stories, an equal number of critical and miscellaneous articles, a philosophic poem *Eureka*, and a purely realistic novel, *The Narrative of Arthur Gordon Pym*. If I have another occasion to speak about this poet, I should offer an analysis of both his philosophical and literary views, and of his works in general, a complete translation of which would run little chance of success with a public that much prefers entertainment and sentiment to the most essential philosophic truths.

[*1856*]

Translated by Raymond Foye

NOTES

Edgar Poe, sa vie et ses oeuvres *(1856) is a reworking of an article of the same title, published in the* Revue de Paris, *March-April, 1852. The text used for the translation is* Curiosités esthétiques l'art romantique et autres oeuvres critiques, *edited by Henri Lemaitre. (Paris: Editions Garnier Frères, 1962).*

1. *Gautier refers to the legend of the eagle who dropped a tortoise on the bald head of Aeschylus, mistaking it for a rock.*
2. *Alfred de Vigny,* Stello.
3. *Joseph de Maistre,* Soirées of St. Petersburg, *IV.*
4. *George Sand, of whom Baudelaire later wrote, "I have read lately a preface in which she writes that the true Christian cannot believe in Hell. She has good reasons for wishing to abolish Hell." (*My Heart Laid Bare, *L.)*
5. *Gérard de Nerval, poet, novelist, and translator, found hanged in the back streets of Paris, 1855.*
6. *Baudelaire dedicated his translations to Poe's mother-in-law, Maria Clemm.*
7. *Another reference to Nerval, who was famous for holding forth among the workers and vagrants of Paris.*
8. *This passage is frequently cited as an anticipation of Proust.*

NEW NOTES ON EDGAR POE[1]
By Charles BAUDELAIRE

I.

Decadent Literature! Empty words we often hear fall, with the resonance of a grandiloquent yawn, from the mouths of sphinxes with no riddle who sit watch on the sacred gates of classical esthetics. Every time this irrefutable oracle sounds, one can be certain that it is for a work more amusing than the Iliad, most likely a poem or a novel whose various parts are arranged to surprise, whose style is magnificently ornate, where all the resources of language and prosody have been used by an impeccable hand. When I hear the roar of anathema—which, I might add in passing, generally falls on some favorite poet, I am forever seized with the desire to respond: "Do you take me for a barbarian as you are, and do you think me capable of occupying myself as miserably? Grotesque similies brew in my head; it is as if two women stand before me: the one, a rustic matron, disgustingly healthy and virtuous, without distinction or character, in short, owing her all to simple nature; the other, one of those beauties who dominate and oppress one's memory, adding elegant dress to her profound charm and natural eloquence, poised, conscious of her regal bearing,—with a speaking voice like a well-tuned instrument, and a thoughtful look, revealing only what it wishes. There would be no doubt of my choice, and yet, for all that, there are pedagogical sphinxes who reproach me for failing to honor the classics. —But, parables aside, I think I should be permitted to ask these sages if they fully comprehend all the vanity and uselessness of their wisdom. The words decadent literature imply a scale of literature—of infancy, childhood, adolescence, etc. The term, in other words, presumes something fatal and providential, like an inescapable decree. All I can comprehend in these academic words, is that it is shameful to obey this law with pleasure, and we are guilty for delighting in our own fate. —The sun which, for a few hours, was pounding everything with its straight white light, will soon flood the Western horizon with myriad colors. In the play of the dying sun, certain poetic spirits will find new delights: they will bring to light dazzling colonnades, cascades of molten metal, blazing paradises, melancholy splendor, the pleasure of regret, all the magic of dreams, all the opium memories. And the setting sun will seem like the marvellous allegory of a soul charged with life, which descends below the horizon with a magnificent lode of thoughts and dreams.

But what these pedants have not realized is that in the course of life, complications and strange circumstances conjoin, quite unforseen by their schoolboy wisdom. Then their incompetent language fails, as in the case of a nation that begins in decadence, just where others end up—a phenomenon which will perhaps multiply with variations.

If, among the immense colonies of this present century a new literature flourishes, it will most certainly produce spiritual exceptions of a nature disconcerting to the academic mind. Young and old at the same time, America babbles and drivels with astonishing glibness. Who can count its poets? They are innumerable. Its blue stockings? They clutter the magazines. Its critics? You can be certain it has pedants worthy of our own at calling the artist back to antique beauty, at grilling a poet or novelist on the morality of his goals and the quality of his intentions. One finds there as here, but even more than here, men of letters who don't know how to spell—a puerile, useless activity; plenty of compilers, hack writers, plagiarists of plagiarists and critics of critics. In this seething mediocrity, in this society in love with material progress,—a scandal with a new twist which brings to light the grandeur of idlers,—in this society avid for amusement, in love with life, but especially a life of thrills, a man has emerged who is great, not only in metaphysical subtlety, in the sinister or bewitching beauty of his conceptions and the rigor of his analysis, but great not least of all as caricature. —Here I must carefully explain; for recently an impudent critic[2] applied, in order to degrade Edgar Poe and weaken the sincerity of my admiration of him, the word *jongleur* which I myself used on the noble poet as a kind of praise.

At the heart of a greedy world, hungry for material things, Poe took flight in dreams. Smothered as he was by the American scene, he wrote in the preface to *Eureka*: "I offer this book to those who put faith in dreams as the only realities!" He was himself an admirable protest, he was one, and he made one *in his own way*. The author who, in the *Colloquy of Monos and Una*, unleashes a torrent of hatred and disgust for democracy, progress, and *civilization*, the very same author who, to rouse the credulous, to charm the gawkers among them, has emphatically proclaimed human sovereignty, and most cleverly fabricated hoaxes flattering to the pride of *modern man*. When seen in this light, Poe appears as a helot who wishes to shame his master. Lastly, to say what I think in the clearest manner possible, Poe was always great, not only in his lofty conceptions, but also as a hoaxer.

II.

For he was never a dupe! —I do not think that the Virginian who wrote placidly in the onrush of democracy: "The people have nothing to do with the laws but to obey them," has ever fallen prey to modern sagacity—and: "The nose of a mob is its imagination; by this at any time it can be quietly led"; and a hundred other passages where mockery rains down, thick and dense as bullets, but nevertheless nonchalant and superior. —The Swedenborgians congratulate him on the *Mesmeric Revelation*, much like those naive visionaries who formerly kept an eye on the author of *Diable Amoureux*[3], as a revealer of their mysteries; they thank him for the great truths which he has just proclaimed,—for they have discovered (O verifiers of the unverifiable!) that all that he has stated is obviously true; although at first, these good people confess, they were suspecting that it might well have been simple fiction. Poe responds that, for his part, he never doubted it.—Need I further cite this brief passage which catches my eye, while leafing through for the hundredth time his amusing *Marginalia*, which are like the secret chambers of his mind: "The enormous multiplication of books in all branches of knowledge is one of the scourges of this age, for it is one of the most serious obstacles to the acquisition of any real knowledge." An aristocrat by nature even more than by birth, a Virginian, a man of the South, a Byron unhinged in this wretched world, who always keeps his philosophic cool, and, whether he defines the nose of the mob, or rails against the fabricators of religions, or scoffs at libraries, he remains what he was and always will be, the true poet,—truth cloaked in a bizarre way, an obvious paradox, who does not want to rub elbows with the crowd, and who runs to the far East when the fireworks go off in the West.

But this is more important than anything: let us note that this author, the product of a century infatuated with itself, the child of a nation more infatuated with itself than any other, has clearly seen, has imperturbably affirmed the wickedness of man. There is within man, he says, a mysterious force that modern philosophy does not wish to take into consideration; and nevertheless, without this unnameable force, without this primordial tendency, a whole array of human actions will remain unexplained, inexplicable. These actions appeal only *because* they are evil, dangerous, having the lure of the abyss. This primitive, irresistible force is a natural Perversity, that makes man at once both a homicide and a suicide, assassin and executioner;—for, he adds, with a remarkably satanic subtlety, the impossibility of finding a reasonable motive for certain depraved and perilous acts might lead us to regard them as suggestions from the Devil, if history and experience did not instruct that God often draws on them to establish order and to punish rogues; *after having employed the same rogues as accomplices!* such is the thought that slips, I confess, into my mind, an implication as treacherous as it is inevitable. But I wish, for the present, to note only the great forgotten truth—the primordial perversity of man,—and not without a certain satisfaction, I witness some of the debris of ancient wisdom returns to us from an unexpected country. It is pleasing that a few old truths have blown up in the faces of all those sycophants of humanity, all of those pollyannas and bores who repeat in all the various possible tones: "I am born good and so are you and everybody born good!" forgetting, no! pretending to forget, these misguided egalitarians, that all of us are born marked with evil!

By what lies could he be duped, he who often—through the sad necessity of his environs—faced them so well? What scorn for pseudo-philosophy, on his good days, on the days when he was, shall we say, illuminated. This poet, several of whose works seem to have been made deliberately to confirm the so-called omnipotence of man, has sometimes wished to purge himself. The day that he wrote 'all certainty is in dreams,' he drove his own Americanism down into the region of inferior things; at other times, returning to the true path of the poet, obeying without a doubt the ineluctable truth that haunts us like a demon, he heaved the passionate sighs of *the fallen angel who remembers Heaven*,[4] lamenting the golden age and the lost Eden; he wept for all the magnificence of nature, *shrivelling up under the fervid breath of the furnaces*; lastly he wrote those admirable pages: *The Colloquy of Monos and Una*, which would have charmed and perturbed the impeccable de Maistre.

It is he who said of socialism, in a time before it had a name, or at least before this name was fully vulgarized: "The world is infested just now by a new sect of philosophers, not yet suspected of forming a sect, and who consequently have no name. They are the *Believers in Worn-Out Ideas*. (One might say, preachers of the obsolete.) Their high priest in the East is Charles Fourier,—in the West, Horace Greeley; and high priests they are to some purpose. The only common bond in the sect is credulity;—let us call it insanity at once and be done with it. Ask any one of them why he believes this or that, and, if he be conscientious (ignorant people generally are), he will make you a reply very much as Talleyrand made when asked why he believed in the Bible. "I believe in it first," he said, "because I am Bishop of Atun; and, secondly, *because I don't understand anything in it.*" What these philosophers call "argument" is a way they have of *denying* Progress; and that great heresy of decrepitude did not escape him either. The reader will see in different passages, the various terms he uses to characterize it. One might truly say, considering the fury he expended, that he had to revenge it as a public nuisance, or as a scourge in the streets. How he would have laughed, with the scornful laugh of the poet who never wastes time with the throngs of idlers, had he stumbled, as I did, upon this marvellous phrase which reminds me of the buffoonish and deliberate absurdities of clowns, and which I discovered perfidiously displayed in a journal of high distinction: *The unceasing progress of science has very recently allowed us to rediscover the long lost secret* (Greek fire, the tempering of copper, any old mystery of the ages) *of which the most successful practice dates back to a barbarous and very ancient epoch!!! Voilà*, a sentence that can be called a real find, a startling discovery even in a century of unceasing progress; but I believe that the mummy Allamistakeo[5] would not have missed a chance to enquire, with a suave and discreet tone of superiority, if it were not also through the grace of *unceasing* progress—fatal and irresistible law of progress—that this famous secret was not lost in the first place. But, aside from joking about this subject, as sad as it is laughable, is it not genuinely stupefying to see a nation, many nations, soon all of humanity, saying to its sages, to its sorcerers: "I shall love you and call you great, if you can assure me that we are progressing in spite of ourselves, inevitably, while we sleep: relieve us of the responsibility, veil humiliating comparisons, adulterate history, and you may call yourself the wisest of the wise??" Is it not astonishing that this simple idea does not dawn on every mind: that progress (to the extent that there is progress) perfects pain in the proportion that it refines pleasure, and that, if the people's skin is getting more delicate, they are evidently on the trail of an *Italiam fugientum*,[6] a conquest lost every minute, a progress which forever negates itself??

But these self-interested illusions originate in the dregs of perversity and deceit—marsh gas—and fill with loathing those souls so in love with eternal fire, like Edgar Poe, and exasperate dim intellects, like Jean-Jacques[7] in whom a wounded sensibility and a readiness to revolt takes the place of philosophy. That he was right in his charge against *the depraved animal*, is incontestable; but the depraved animal has the right to reproach him for invoking simple nature. Nature produces only monsters, and the whole question lies in the examination of the word *savages*. No philosopher would dare propose as models those wretched, diseased hordes, victims of the elements, food for beasts, as incapable of producing arms as conceiving of the idea of a supreme, spiritual power. But, if one wishes to compare modern man, civilized man, with man the savage, or rather a so-called civilized nation with a so-called savage nation, that is to say deprived of all of the ingenious inventions which supplant individual heroism, who could fail to see that all honor belongs to the savage? By his nature, by necessity itself, he is encyclopedic, while civilized man finds himself confined to the infinitely paltry regions of his own specialization. Civilized man invents the philosophy of progress to console himself for his abdication and his downfall; while the primitive man, a feared and respected husband, a warrior of personal gallantry, a poet of the melancholy hours when the setting sun induces songs of the past and of his ancestors, nears the edge of the idea. With what inadequacy can we reproach him? He has the priest, magician and doctor. What more? He has the dandy, the supreme incarnation of the idea of the beautiful transported to material life, he who sets style and arbitrates manners. His clothing, his adornments, his weapons, his pipe, give proof of an inventive faculty that has long since deserted us. Shall we compare our tired eyes and our deafened ears to those eyes which pierce the mist, to those ears *that would hear the grass growing*? And the primitive woman of simple and childlike soul, an obedient and endearing animal, giving herself entirely and knowing that she is only half a destiny, shall we declare her inferior to the American lady whom M. Bellegarigue[8] (editor of the *Grocer's Bulletin!*) believed he was praising when he said that she was the ideal of the kept woman? This same woman, whose mundane manners inspired Edgar Poe—so gallant, so respectful of beauty—to pen these sad lines: "The large purses, resembling gigantic cucumbers, which have come into vogue among our belles, are *not* of Parisian origin as many suppose, but are strictly indigenous. The fact is, such a fashion would be quite out of place in Paris, where it is money *only* that women keep in a purse. The purse of an American lady, however, must be large enough to carry both her money and the soul of its owner." As for religion, I shall not speak of Vitzilipoutzli as flippantly as Alfred Musset did: I say without shame that I much prefer the cult of the Tetuatès[9] to that of Mammon: and the priest who offers to the cruel extortioner of human sacrifice victims who die *honorably*, victims who *want* to die seems to me far more pleasing and humane, compared to the financier who immolates whole populations in his interest alone. Now and then, these things are half-seen, and I once uncovered in an article by M. Barbey d'Aurevilly an exclamation of philosophical gloom which, in short, is all I wish to say about this matter:—"Civilized people, forever casting stones at savages, soon you will not even deserve to be idolaters!"

Such a world, as I have previously said, and cannot but reiterate, is scarcely made for poets. What the French intellect, supposedly the most democratic, understands by a State, would not be understood by the American mind. For every intellect of the old world, a political state is a hub of activities which is its brain and its sun, having glorious and ancient memories, long poetic and military annals, an aristocracy, to which poverty, the daughter of revolutions, can only contribute a paradoxical luster; but that! that mob of buyers and sellers, nameless, that headless monster, that outcast on the other side of the Ocean, a State! Very well then, if a vast barroom where the customers throng and conduct affairs at soiled tables, amid the din of coarse talk, if that can be compared to a *salon*, to what we used to call a salon, a republic of mind presided over by beauty!

It will always be difficult to exist, nobly and productively, as a man of letters, without facing defamation, slander by the impotent, the envy of the rich, that envy which is their punishment!—or the vengeance of bourgeois mediocrity. But what is difficult in a restrained monarchy or in a regular republic, becomes nearly impossible in a kind of lumber yard where every town sergeant polices his own opinions to the profit of his own vices—or his own virtues, for they are one and the same;—where a poet or novelist in a slave society is a detestable writer in the eyes of an abolitionist critic, where one does not know which is the greater scandal, sloppy cynicism or imperturbable Biblical hypocrisy. Burning shackled Negroes, guilty for having felt their dark cheeks thrill with an honorable blush, playing with revolvers in the pit of a theater, establishing polygamy in the paradise of the West, which the savages (a term with an air of injustice) had not yet soiled with these shameful utopias, advertising on the walls, no doubt, to consecrate the principle of unbounded liberty, *the cure for nine-month illnesses*, such are a few of the salient qualities, some moral examples from the noble nation of Franklin, inventor of a counting-house morality, the hero of a country dedicated to materialism. It is well to reflect on these crude marvels at a time when Americanomania has become nearly a passion of the times, to the point where an archbishop has promised, straight-faced, that Providence would soon call on us to enjoy this transatlantic ideal.

III.

Such a social milieu necessarily engenders corresponding literary errors. Against these errors, Poe reacted as often as possible, and with full force. We should not be surprised then that American writers, while recognizing his singular power as a poet and storyteller, have always denied his merit as a critic. In a country where the idea of utility, the most hostile in the world to the idea of beauty, supercedes and dominates everything, the perfect critic will be the most *honorable*, that is, one whose inclinations and desires most resemble the inclinations and desires of hispublic,—one who, confusing the ways and means of production, assigns to all a single goal,—the one who will seek in a book of poetry the means of perfecting conscience. Naturally, it follows that he will be all the less concerned with the real, positive beauties of poetry; he will be all the less shocked by the imperfections and even the flaws of execution. Edgar Poe, to the contrary, dividing the world of the mind into *pure intellect, taste,* and *moral sense*, applied the critique of the object of his analysis in accordance with one of these three divisions. He was, above all, sensitive to perfection of plan and to exactness of execution; disassembling literary works like defective pieces of machinery (relative to their aims), meticulously noting the flaws of fabrication; and, when he came to the particulars of the work, to its plastic expression, in a word, to its style, he examined, without omission, the faults of prosody, the errors in grammar, and all of the accumulated dross which, among writers who are not artists, foul the best intentions and deform even the most noble conceptions.

For him, imagination is the queen of the faculties, but by this word he understands something greater than what is understood by the common reader. The imagination is not fantasy; nor is it sensibility, although it would be difficult to conceive of an imaginative man who was not sensitive. The imagination is a quasi-divine faculty that perceives all at once, beyond philosophical methods, the secret meaning of things, their correspondences and analogies. The honors and province he confers on this faculty give it such merit (at least when the thoughts of the author have been well understood), that the scholar without imagination seems only a counterfeit scholar, or at least incomplete.

Among the domains of literature where imagination can obtain the most curious results, can harvest not the richest treasures, nor the most precious (those belong to poetry), but the most numerous and the most varied, there is one Poe liked particularly—the short story. It has an immense advantage over the novel of vast proportions in that its brevity adds to the intensity of effect. This kind of reading, which can be done in one sitting, leaves a keener recollection in the mind than a broken reading, interrupted by business worries and worldly interests. The unity of impression, the totality of effect, is an immense advantage which can give this genre of writing an altogether unique superiority, to the point that a short story too brief (this is doubtless a fault) is preferable to one too long. The artist, if he is skillful, will not accommodate his ideas to the incidents; but, having conceived deliberately and unhurriedly, an effect he desires to produce, will invent incidents, will combine the events most fitting to induce the desired effect. If the first sentence is not written with an eye toward providing this final impression, the work is deficient from the start. In the whole composition, not a single, unintentional word must slip in, that does not tend, directly or indirectly, to perfect the preconceived design.

There is one point on which the short story is superior even to the poem. Rhythm is necessary to the development of the idea of beauty, which is the greatest and noblest aim of the poem. Now the artifices of rhythm are an insurmountable obstacle in the exacting development of thought and expression, whose object is *truth*. For truth can often be the aim of the short story, and reasoning the best tool for the construction of the perfect short story. That is why this type of composition, though not so greatly exalted as pure poetry, can furnish more varied results. more easily appreciated by the ordinary reader. Furthermore, the author of a short story has at his disposal a multitude of tones, nuances of language; the rational tone, the sarcastic, the humorous, which poetry repudiates and which appear as dissonances, as outrages to the idea of pure beauty. And that is why an author who pursues in a short story the simple aim of beauty, works at a great disadvantage, deprived of the instrument of greatest utility, rhythm. I know that, in the whole of literature, efforts have been made, sometimes auspicious, to create purely poetic tales; Edgar Poe himself has written beautiful ones. But they are struggles and efforts which only serve to demonstrate the strength of the true means adopted to corresponding goals, and I am inclined to believe that, in some authors, the greatest of them, these heroic attempts spring from despair.

IV.

"*Genus irritabile vatum.*[10] That poets (using the word comprehensively, as including artists in general) are a 'genus irritabile,' is well understood; but the *why*, seems not to be commonly seen. An artist *is* an artist only by dint of his exquisite sense of Beauty—a sense affording him rapturous enjoyment, but at the same time implying, or involving, an equally exquisite sense of Deformity or disproportion. Thus a wrong—an injustice—done a poet who is really a poet, excites him to a degree which, to ordinary apprehension, appears *disproportionate* with the wrong. Poets see injustice—*never* where it does not exist—but very often where the unpoetical see no injustice whatever. Thus the poetical irritability has no reference to '*temper*' in the vulgar sense, but merely to a more than usual clear-sightedness in respect to Wrong:—this clear sightedness being nothing more than a corollary to the vivid perception of Right—of justice—of proportion—in a word, of the beautiful. But one thing is clear—that the man who is not '*irritabile*,' (to the ordinary apprehension), is no poet."

Thus the poet himself speaks, readying an excellent and irrefutable apologia for all those of his race. Poe carried this sensibility into literary affairs, and the extreme importance he attached to all things poetic often induced in him a tone which, in the judgement of the weak, smacked of superiority. I believe that I have previously remarked that many of the prejudices which he had to combat, the twisted notions, the vulgar ideas which circulated around him, have for a long time infected the French press. It will not be futile then to give a brief summary of some of his most important opinions about poetic composition. The parallelism of error will make for easy application.

But I must say above all, that aside from a natural and innate poetic gift, Poe valued science, work and analysis to a degree seemingly exorbitant to the haughty and unknowledgeable. Not only has he expended considerable effort on surrendering the fugitive demon of happier moments to his will, summoning up those exquisite sensations. those spiritual hungers, those states of poetic well-being, so rare, so precious as to be really thought of as a state of grace foreign to man, and as visitations; what is more he has subjected inspiration to method, to the severest analysis. The choice of means! he repeats this unceasingly, he insists with scholarly eloquence on making means appropriate to effects, on the use of rhyme, on perfecting the refrain, on adapting rhythm to emotion. He asserted that he who cannot seize the intangible is no poet; that he alone is a poet who is master of his memory, the sovereign of words, the register of his own feelings always open for inspection. All for the *dénouement!* he so often repeats. Even a sonnet requires a plan, and its construction, the framework, so to speak, is the most important guarantee of the mysterious life of the works of the mind.

Naturally I turn to an article entitled: *The Poetic Principle*[11], and I find, from the outset, a vigorous protest against what could be called, in matters of poetry, the heresy of length or dimension,—the absurd value attached to long poems. "I hold that a long poem does not exist. I maintain that the long poem is a flat contradiction in terms." In effect, a poem merits that name only so far as it excites, as it elevates the soul, and the positive value of a poem is in ratio to this excitation, to this elevation of the soul. But, out of psychological necessity, all excitations are fugitive and transitory. This singular state, into which the reader's soul has been drawn, as if by force, will certainly not endure as long as the reading of any poem exceeds the tenacious enthusiasm of which human nature is capable.

It is evident then the epic poem stands condemned. For a work of this dimension can be considered poetic only to the extent that it sacrifices a condition vital to every work of art, unity:—I do not speak of unity of conception, but unity of impression, of the *totality* of effect, as I said earlier when I compared the novel with the short story. The epic poem appears to us then, esthetically speaking, as a paradox. It is possible that ancient eras have produced series of lyric poems, later linked by compilers into epic poems; but every *epic intention* is clearly the result of an imperfect sense of art. The time for these artistic anomalies has passed, and it is even doubtful that a long poem has ever been truly popular in the full sense of the word.

It must be added that a poem too short, one that does not provide a *pabulum* equal to the excitement created, one that is not on a level with the reader's natural appetite, is also very defective. However brilliant and intense the effect, it does not last; the memory does not retain it; it is like a seal which, pressed too lightly and too hastily has not had time to imprint its image on the wax.

But there is yet another heresy, which, thanks to hypocrisy, the loutishness and baseness of men's minds, is far more formidable and stands a greater chance of survival—an error even more long-lived,—I speak of the heresy of *the didactic*, which includes as inevitable corollaries the heresies of *passion*, of *truth*, and of *morality*. A great many people think the aim of poetry is some sort of lesson, that it must now fortify the conscience, now *demonstrate* the utility of something or other. Edgar Poe maintains that Americans especially have sponsored this heterodox idea; alas! there is no need to go as far as Boston to encounter the heresy in question. Even here, it besieges us, and it batters true poetry every day. Poetry, if one is willing to descend into one's self, interrogate the soul, and invoke memories of enthusiams, has no other end but itself; it can have no other, and no poem will be so great, so noble, so genuinely worthy of the name of poetry, as the one written expressly for the pleasure of writing a poem.

I do not mean to say that poetry does not ennoble manners—let this be understood—that its final result is not to elevate man above the level of commonplace affairs; that would be an obvious absurdity. I say that, if the poet has pursued a moral aim, he has diminished his poetic force; and it is not rash to wager that his work will be bad. Poetry cannot, under penalty of death or failure, be equated with morality; Truth is not its object, it has only itself. The modes for demonstrating truth are other and elsewhere. Truth has nothing to do with song. All that makes the charm, the grace, the allure of song, would strip truth of its authority and power. Cold, calm, impassive, the demonstrative humor refuses the diamonds and flowers of the Muse; it is then absolutely the inverse of the poetic humor.

The pure intellect aims at truth, taste reveals beauty to us, and moral sense teaches us duty. It is true that the sense of taste is intimately connected with the two extremes, and it is separated from moral sense by a difference so slight, that Aristotle did not hesitate to classify some of its delicate operations among the virtues. Thus, what particularly exasperates the man of taste in the spectacle of vice is its deformity, its disproportion. Vice endangers the right and true, revolts the intellect and the conscience; but, as an outrage to harmony, as dissonance, it wounds most particularly certain poetic spirits; and I do not believe it scandalous to consider every infraction against morality, against moral beauty, as a kind of insult against universal rhythm and prosody.

It is this admirable and immortal instinct for the beautiful which causes us to consider the earth and its wonders as a revelation, as a correspondence with Heaven. The insatiable thirst for all that lies beyond, and what life reveals, is the most vital proof of our immortality. It is at once by poetry and *through* poetry, by and *through* music, that the soul glimpses the splendors beyond the tomb; and, when we are moved to tears by an exquisite poem, those tears are not the result of excessive joy, they are instead testimony to an inflamed melancholy, demanding nerves, a nature exiled in imperfection, and which seeks to possess, at once, on this very earth, a paradise revealed.

Thus, the poetic principle is strictly and simply the human aspiration toward a superior beauty, and the manifestation of this principle is an enthusiasm, an excitation of soul—an enthusiasm altogether independent of passion, which is an intoxication of the heart, and of truth, which is the bread of reason. For passion is *natural*, too natural not to introduce an impaired, discordant tone into the domain of pure beauty, too familiar and too violent not to scandalize pure desires, the graceful melancholies and noble despairs that inhabit the supernatural regions of poetry.

This extraordinary elevation, this exquisite delicacy, and this accent of immortality that Edgar Poe demands of the Muse, far from making him less attentive to the practice of writing have pushed him always to sharpen his genius as a practitioner. Many people, particularly those who have read the strange poem entitled *The Raven*, would be shocked if I were to analyze the article in which our poet, seemingly in innocence, but with a slight impertinence which I cannot fault, explains in minute detail the method of construction he employed, the adaptation of rhythm, the choice of a refrain,—the shortest possible, the most susceptible to a variety of applications, and at the same time the most representative of melancholy and despair, embellished with the most sonorous rhyme of all (*nevermore, jamais plus*),—the choice of a bird capable of imitating the human voice, but a bird—the raven—branded in popular imagination as a baneful and fatal character,—the choice of the most poetic of all tones, the melancholic,—the most poetic sentiment, the love for a dead beloved, etc. "And I shall not place," he says, "the hero of my poem in poor surroundings, because poverty is coarse and contrary to the idea of beauty. His melancholy shall reside in a room magnificently and poetically furnished." The reader will detect in many of Poe's short stories the curious signs of this inordinate taste for beautiful and strange forms, for ornate surroundings and oriental sumptuousness.

I said that this article seemed to me blemished by a slight impertinence. The partisans of inspiration would not fail to find it a blasphemy and profanation; but I believe it is expressly for them that this article was written. Just as certain writers affect abandon, aiming for a masterpiece with their eyes shut, full of confidence in disorder, expecting that words thrown to the ceiling will fall back down as poems on the floor, so Edgar Poe—one of the most inspired men I know—made a pretense of hiding spontaneity, of simulating cold deliberation. "I believe I can boast," he said with an amused pride I don't find in bad taste, "that no one point in its composition was left either to chance or intuition—and that the whole work proceeded, step by step, to its completion with the precision and rigid consequence of a mathematical problem." There are none, I say, but the lovers of chance, the fatalists of inspiration, and the fanatics of *free verse* who can find this *minutiae* bizarre. There are no minutiae in matters of art.

Apropos of free verse, I would add that Poe attached an extreme importance to rhyme, and that, in the analysis he made of the mathematical and musical pleasure the mind derives from rhyme, he has brought as much care, as much subtlety as in all the other subjects relating to the craft of poetry. Just as he showed that the refrain is susceptible to an infinite variety of applications, he has also sought to rejuvenate it, to double the pleasure of rhyme by adding an unexpected element, *strangeness*, which is the indispensable condiment of all beauty. He frequently makes happy use of repetitions of the same line or of several lines, a persistent refrain of phrases which simulate the obsessions of melancholy or of an *idée fixe*—of a refrain pure and simple, but used in many different ways—of a variant-refrain which suggests indolence and distraction—of double and triple rhymes, and also a kind of rhyme that introduces into modern poetry, but with more precision and intention, the surprises of Leontine verse.[12]

It is evident that the value of all these means can only be verified through use; and a translation of poetry so deliberate, so concentrated, can be a soothing dream, but it is only a dream. Poe wrote little poetry; he sometimes expressed regret not to be able to devote himself, not just more often, but exclusively, to the kind of work he considered noblest. But his poetry is always powerful in impact. It is not the fervent effusions of Byron, nor the soft, harmonious, and distinguished melancholy of Tennyson, for whom, moreover, he had a semi-fraternal admiration. It is something profound and dazzling like a dream, mysterious and perfect like crystal. I need not add, I presume, that American critics have often denigrated his poetry; very recently, I found in an American biographical dictionary, an article which disparaged its strangeness, expressed fear that this muse in the dress of wisdom might attract a school in the glorious country of utilitarian morality, and finally regretted that Poe did not apply his talents to the expression of moral truths instead of expending them in quest of a bizarre ideal, and of lavishing on his verses a mysterious, albeit sensual, voluptuousness.

We are all acquainted with these shifting attacks. The reproaches heaped upon good poets by bad critics are the same in every country. In reading this article, it seemed to me I was reading the translation of one of the numerous indictments by the Parisian critics of those poets of ours who are most devoted to perfection. Our preferences are easily surmised, and every lover of pure poetry will understand me when I say that among our antipoetic race, Victor Hugo would be less admired if he were perfect, and he has been exonerated for his lyric genius only by introducing into his poetry, forcefully and brutally, what Edgar Poe considered the prime modern heresy: *the didactic.*

[1857]

Translated by Raymond Foye

NOTES

1. Notes nouvelles sur Edgar Poe *was published in March, 1857 as the introduction to the second volume of Poe translations. Text: Editions Garnier.*
2. *Barbey d'Aurevilly,* Le Pays *(June 10, 1856).*
3. *Jacques Cazotte, executed in 1792.*
4. *Baudelaire paraphrases the popular lines of Lamartine, "L'homme est un dieu tombé, qui se souvient des cieux!"*
5. *Cf. Poe's popular tale "Some Words with a Mummy."*
6. *Virgil,* Aeneid.
7. *Jean Jacques Rousseau.*
8. *M. Bellegarigue published a popular book in 1853 in Paris entitled "The Women of America."*
9. *The name of an Aztec god in a work by Alfred de Musset.*
10. *"The irascible race of poets." Horace,* Epistles, *II, 2, 102.*
11. *This essay, written in the last years of his life, was Poe's credo. It is frequently anthologized. (Baudelaire quotes from it freely, as well as from "The Philosophy of Composition," in which Poe describes the methods by which he claimed to have written "The Raven.")*
12. *A form of internal rhyme characterized by the rhyming of the syllable preceding the caesura with the last syllable of the line.*

Self-portrait by Baudelaire after smoking hashish

From A REBOURS
By J. K. HUYSMANS

To enjoy a literature uniting, as he desired, with an incisive style, a penetrating, feline power of analysis, he must resort to that master of Induction, that strange, profound thinker, Edgar Allan Poe, for whom, since the moment when he had begun to re-read him, his predilection had suffered no possible diminution.

Better than any other writer perhaps, Poe possessed those close affinities of spirit that fulfilled the demands Des Esseintes had formulated in the course of his meditations.

While Baudelaire had deciphered in the hieroglyphics of the soul the period of recurrence of feeling and thoughts, *he* had, in the realm of morbid psychology, more particularly scrutinized the region of will.

In literature, he had been the first, under the emblematic title of "The Imp of the Perverse," to explore those irresistible impulses which the will submits to without understanding their nature and which cerebral pathology now accounts for with a fair degree of certainty; again, he was the first, if not to note, at any rate to make generally known, the depressing influence of fear acting on the will, like those anaesthetics that paralyze sensibility and that *curare* that annihilates the nervous elements of motion; it was on this point, this lethargy of the will, that he had focused his studies, analyzing the effects of this moral poison, pointing out the symptoms of its progress, the troubles incidental to it, beginning with anxiety, proceeding to anguish, culminating finally in terror which stupefies the powers of volition, yet without the intelligence, however severely shaken, actually giving way.

To death, which the dramatists had so lavishly abused, he had, in a manner, given a new and keener edge, made other than it was, introducing into it an algebraic and superhuman element; yet, to say truly, it was not so much the actual death agony of the dying he depicted as the moral agony of the survivor, haunted before the bed of suffering by the monstrous hallucinations engendered by pain and fatigue. With a hideous fascination he concentrated his gaze on the effects of terror, on the collapse of the will; applied to these horrors the cold light of reason; little by little choking the breath out of the throat of the reader who pants and struggles, suffocated before these mechanically reproduced nightmares of raging fever.

Convulsed by hereditary nervous disorders, maddened by moral choreas, his characters lived only by the nerves; his women, the Morellas, the Ligeias, possessed a vast erudition, deeply imbued with the foggy mists of German metaphysics and the cabalistic mysteries of the ancient East; all had the inert bosoms of boys or angels, all were, so to say, unsexual.

Baudelaire and Poe, whose minds have often been compared because of their common poetical inspiration and the predilection they shared for the examination of mental maladies, yet differed radically in their conceptions of love,—and these conceptions filled a large place in their works. Baudelaire's passion was a thirsty, ruthless thing, a thing of cruel disillusion that suggested only reprisals and tortures; Poe's a matter of chaste and ethereal amours, where the senses had no existence, and the brain alone was stirred to erethism with nothing to correspond in the bodily organs, which, if they existed at all, remained forever frozen and virgin.

This cerebral clinic where, vivisecting in a stifling atmosphere, this spiritual surgeon became, directly his attention flagged, the prey of his imagination, which sprayed about him, like delicious miasmas, apparitions whether of nightmare horrors or of angelic hosts, was for Des Esseintes a source of indefatigable conjectures. Now, however, when his nerves were all sick and on edge, there were days when such reading exhausted him, days when it left him with trembling hands and ears strained and watchful, feeling himself, like the lamentable Usher, seized by unreasoning pangs of dread, by a secret terror.

So he felt bound to moderate his zeal, to indulge sparingly in these formidable elixirs, just as he now could no longer visit with impunity his red vestibule and intoxicate himself with the sight of Odilon Redon's gloomy paintings or Jan Luyken's representations of tortures.

And yet, when he was in these dispositions of mind, all literature struck him as vapid after these terrible philtres imported from America. [*1884*]

ON POE from SITUATION DE BAUDELAIRE
By Paul VALERY

Before Poe the problem of literature had never been examined in its premises, reduced to a psychological problem, and approached by means of an analysis that deliberately used logic and the mechanics of effect. For the first time the relationship between the work and the reader was made clear and proposed as the actual foundation of art. His analysis—and this circumstance assures us of its value—can be applied and just as clearly verified in every kind of literary production. The same observations, the same distinctions, the same quantitative remarks, the same guiding ideas can be adapted with equal success to works meant to act powerfully and crudely on the sensibility and win an audience that likes strong emotions or strange adventures, as to the most refined types of literature and the delicate organization of the products of the poet's mind.

To say that this analysis holds good for both the tale and the poem, that it applies to the construction of the imaginary and the fantastic as it does to the reconstitution and literary representation of an apparent reality, indicates that its scope is remarkable. What distinguishes a truly general law is its fertility. To reach a point which allows us to dominate a whole field of activity necessarily means that one perceives a quantity of possibilities—unexplored domains, roads to be traced, land to be exploited, cities to be built, relations to be established, processes to be extended. It is therefore not surprising that Poe, possessing so effective and sure a method, became the inventor of several different literary forms; that he provided the first and most striking examples of the scientific tale, of a modern cosmogonic poem, of the novel of criminal investigation, of literature that portrays morbid psychological states; and that all his work presents on every page the act and exigency of an intelligence the like of which is not to be observed to the same degree in any other literary career.

This great man would today be completely forgotten if Baudelaire had not taken up the task of introducing him into European literature. Let us not fail to observe here that Poe's universal fame is dimmed or dubious only in his native country and in England. This Anglo-Saxon poet is strangely neglected by his fellow countrymen.

We may make a further observation: *Baudelaire and Edgar Allan Poe exchanged values.* Each gave to the other what he had, and received from the other what he had not. One communicated to the other a whole system of new and profound thought. He enlightened him, enriched him, determined his opinions on a number of subjects: the philosophy of composition, the theory of the artificial, the comprehension and condemnation of the modern, the importance of the exceptional and of a certain strangeness, an aristocratic attitude, mystical fervor, a taste for elegance and precision, even politics . . . Every aspect of Baudelaire was impregnated, inspired, deepened by Poe.

But, in exchange for what he had taken, Baudelaire gave Poe's thought an infinite expanse. He offered it to future generations. That transcendence which changes the poet into himself, as in Mallarmé's great line,* this was what Baudelaire's action, his translations, his prefaces, assured for the miserable shade of Edgar Allan Poe.

**Tel qu'en Lui-même enfin l'éternité le change. . . .*
To what he was in himself eternity transforms him. . . .

I shall not go into everything that literature owes to the influence of this marvellous inventor. Whether we take Jules Verne and his disciples, Gaboriau and the like, or whether, at far more sophisticated levels, we recall the productions of Villiers de l'Isle-Adam or of Dostoevsky, it is easy to see that the *Narrative of Arthur Gordon Pym, Murders in the Rue Morgue, Ligeia*, the *Tell-Tale Heart*, are models that have been abundantly imitated, thoroughly studied, and never surpassed.

I shall merely ask myself what Baudelaire's poetry, and more generally French poetry, may owe to the discovery of the works of Poe.

Some poems in *Les Fleurs du Mal* derive their sentiment and their substance from Poe's poems. Some contain lines which are exact transpositions; but I shall ignore these particular borrowings, the importance of which is, in a way, merely local.

I shall concentrate on the essential, that is to say, the very idea Poe had formed of poetry. His conception, which he set forth in various articles, was the principal factor in the modification of Baudelaire's ideas and art. The ramifications of this theory of composition in Baudelaire's mind, the lessons he deduced from it, the developments it received from his intellectual posterity—and above all its great intrinsic value—require us to pause a little to examine it.

I will not deny that Poe's reflections are founded on a certain metaphysical system he forged for himself. But this system, if it directs and dominates and suggests the theories in question, by no means penetrates them. It engenders them and explains their generation; it does not constitute them.

His ideas on poetry are expressed in a few essays, the most important (and the one which least concerns the technique of English verse) being entitled "The Poetic Principle."

Baudelaire was so deeply moved by this essay, he received so intense an impression from it, that he considered its contents—and not merely the contents but the form itself—*as his own property.*

Men cannot help appropriating what seems so exactly made *for them* that, in spite of themselves, they look on it as being made *by them.* . . . They tend irresistibly to take over what suits their own person so closely; and in the very word *good*, language itself confounds the notion of what is adapted to someone and satisfies him entirely with what is a man's possessions.

Now although Baudelaire was enlightened and obsessed by the theory contained in "The Poetic Principle"—or, rather, just because he was enlightened and obsessed by it—he did not include a translation of this essay in Poe's own works, but introduced the most interesting part of it, scarcely altered and with the sentence order changed, into the preface he wrote for his translation of the *Tales*. This plagiarism would be open to discussion of its author had not himself, as we shall see, drawn attention to it: in an article on Théophile Gautier he reproduced the whole passage in question, and prefaced it with these very clear and surprising lines: "It is on occasion permissible, I believe, to quote from one's own writings in order to avoid self-paraphrase. I shall therefore repeat. . . ." The borrowed passage follows.

What then were Poe's views on poetry?

I shall sum up his ideas briefly. He analyzes the psychological conditions of a poem. In the first rank he puts those conditions that depend on the *dimensions* of poetical works. He gives singular importance to the considerations of their length. He also examines the very substance of these compositions. He easily establishes that there exist a great number of poems concerned with notions for which prose would have been an adequate vehicle. Neither history, science, nor morality gains when it is expounded in the language of the soul. Didactic, historical, or ethical poetry, although exemplified and consecrated by the greatest poets, combines the alien materials of discursive or empirical knowledge with the creations of the secret sensibility and the forces of passion.

Poe saw that modern poetry was destined to conform to the tendency of an age which has witnessed an increasingly sharp distinction between the modes and provinces of human activity; and that it could now entertain claim to attain its true object and produce itself, as it were, in a *pure state*.

Thus, having analyzed the conditions for poetic enjoyment, and defined *pure poetry* by way of *elimination*, Poe was opening up a way, teaching a very strict and deeply alluring doctrine, in which a kind of mathematics and a kind of mysticism became one. . . .

[*1924*]

Translated by James R. Lawler

RESPONSES TO INQUIRIES
By Stéphane MALLARME

I revere Poe's judgment—no trace of a philosophy, ethic, or metaphysic will show through; I add that it must be so, inclusive and latent. To avoid some reality of structure remaining around this spontaneous and magical architecture does not imply a lack of powerful and subtle calculations, but they are not apparent; they happen on their own, deliberately mysterious. The song springs from an inborn source; anterior to a concept, so purely as to reflect, outside, a thousand rhythms of images. What genius for being a poet! What lightning instinct to simply enclose life, virgin, in its synthesis and far illuminating everything. The intellectual framework of the poem hides—and exists—in the space that isolates the strophes in the white of the paper: significant silence no less beautiful to create than the verse.

SOME MEDALLIONS AND FULL-LENGTH PORTRAITS
From PORTRAITS OF THE NEXT CENTURY
By Stéphane MALLARME

Edgdar Poe was revealed to me personally after Whistler. I knew—defying marble—that forehead, those eyes with the depth of a star denied only distance, a mouth that every snake except laughter twisted; sacred as a portrait before a volume of works, but the demon full-length! His tragic black seductiveness, unquiet and discreet: the person analogous to the painter—for whomever encounters him at this time in our country, even to the preciosity of his method of handling his material—speaks to the same state of American rarefaction toward beauty. Villiers de l'Isle-Adam, on some nights, in evening dress, young or superior, evoked the whole silent Shadow. However, and to tell the truth, in spite of my confronting daguerreotypes and engravings, a special devotion enjoins my representing the pure among Spirits—rather than as, and in preference to, a person—as an aerolith: starlike, of lightning, projected from completed human designs, very far today from us to whom he bursts into jewels for a crown for someone many a century from now. He is that exception, in fact: and the absolute literary phenomenon.

EDGAR POE from ANTHOLOGIE DE L'HUMOUR NOIR
By André BRETON

Regardless of what may have been, according to his "Philosophy of Composition," Edgar Poe's major claim: to make the accomplishment of the work of art depend upon a prior methodic organization of its elements in view of the effect to be produced, one must admit that he often abandoned this rigor to give, in his work, free reign to fantasy. Whatever may have been said his taste for the artificial and the extraordinary must have swept away his analytic will in many cases: it would be difficult to imagine that that lover of Chance would not have loved to reckon with the chances of expression. We remember the specious distinction that, in his conversation, twenty years ago, Mr. Paul Valéry tried to establish between the "strange" and the "bizarre." The former alone found favor in his eyes, Poe being naturally included in that category. He criticized others, like Jarry, for their attempts at exterior singularity. But, in him whom Mallarmé described as "the demon full length! his tragic black coquetry, unquiet and discreet," it is not wrong to recognize, when the mood strikes, as did Apollinaire on his part, "the marvellous drunkard of Baltimore." "Literary rancors, the vertigo of the infinite, domestic woes, the insults of poverty"—Poe, says Baudelaire, fled into the total darkness of drunkenness, as into the dark of the tomb; for he drank not greedily, but barbarously . . . In New York, the very morning that *The Whig* published "The Raven," while the name of Poe was on everyone's lips, and while everyone argued about his poem, he crossed Broadway staggering against houses and stumbling." Such a contradiction would be enough, in itself, to generate humor, whether it burst nervously from the conflict between exceptional logical facilities, full-dress intellectualism and the mists of drunkenness (*The Angel of the Odd*) or whether, in its most tenebrous form, it lurks around the human inconsistencies which certain morbid states reveal (*The Imp of the Perverse*).

[*1940*]

Translated by John Talbot Hawkes